POLITICAL HUMANITY

Jasmine Ray

with contributions from Kimberly Peticolas and Jayyiah Coles

contents

To all who still believe in humanity, even when it's complicated.

In memory of my brother Jonathan - may you rest in eternal peace.

Sunrise October 12, 1993

Sunset October 24, 2009

INTRODUCTION

There's something almost magical about a child's naiveté. A monumental, life-changing event could unfold right before them, yet their innocence acts as a shield, keeping them blissfully unaware that history is being made. But that same shield, which protects them from the weight of the world, can also prevent them from grasping its significance. Sometimes, it's a gift. Other times, it's a veil, keeping them from seeing the importance of the moment until years later.

I was no different. Like most children, I lived in the present, unaware of the weight of history unfolding around me. I didn't yet understand how moments became milestones, how a name etched onto a street sign could mean more than just words on metal. On that day, as I stood on the other side of the rope, separated from the gathered crowd, I scanned the faces around me. Some were filled with pride, respect, and honor; others were wet with tears, overcome with emotion.

It was April 1991. My mother, my father, Sandy F. Ray III, my brother Jason, and I attended the street-naming ceremony honoring my great-grandfather, the Honorable Reverend Dr. Sandy F. Ray.

Great Grandpa Ray was a visionary and a force of unwavering faith, far more than just a reverend. A dedicated advocate for civil rights, he spent his life not only preaching but actively building pathways to justice. Over time, his church, Cornerstone Baptist Church in Brooklyn, grew to over 5,500 members. But his influence extended far beyond the pulpit.

In 1944, once the congregation outgrew its space, he led the bold acquisition and transformation of a local church into Cornerstone's new home in Bedford-Stuyvesant, a defining act of vision and permanence. He later expanded the church's reach with the creation of an educational center. His decisions shaped not only a congregation but also left a lasting imprint on Brooklyn itself.

Outside of Brooklyn, Reverend Dr. Ray was the first Black representative elected to the Ohio State Legislature. He paved the way for others in politics. He was a founding member of the board of directors for the Gandhi Society for Human Rights, standing alongside many giants of justice. From 1968 to 1979, he served as Vice President of the National Baptist Convention, a testament to the respect he commanded in the faith community. He also served as President of the Empire Missionary Baptist Convention from 1954 to 1979, solidifying his legacy as a leader in both faith and public service.

At eight years old, impatience bubbled inside me as I scanned the crowd. I wasn't thinking about the importance of the day or why we were there. I just knew I hated being dressed up. I was a tomboy, even then, and the whole ordeal—doing my hair, wearing stockings, a skirt, and those stiff, uncomfortable dress shoes—was the absolute worst.

But I did love the red carpet. Cornerstone was known for its bright, bold carpet that ran throughout the church, and I remember sprinting down it like royalty. Because honestly, who was going to stop the great-granddaughter of Rev. Dr. Sandy F. Ray from running in church? No one ever did. And when it came time to eat, I never waited in line. I went straight to the front, another quiet perk of the legacy I carried.

Just as I was about to tug on my mom's dress and ask when lunch was, a sudden gust of wind swept through the air. The April breeze felt different that day—almost alive, almost intentional. My eyes locked on the way it danced through the leaves, lifting them effortlessly and setting them adrift like whispers from another time.

Drawn to it, I followed the wind's path, watching as a single leaf spiraled downward and landed gently at my feet. I bent down and picked it up, running my fingers along its edges—worn, delicate, yet still strong. It wasn't like any leaf I had held before. Its veins stretched across the surface like stories etched in time, reminding me of the veins on our hands, weathered by age yet rich with memory, carrying generations within them. Both silent storytellers. Its color was faded, yet full of history. I couldn't shake the feeling that it had been waiting for me.

Suddenly, I wasn't just standing on a Brooklyn street anymore. As voices around me spoke with pride, honoring the past, I was transported to the very time they described—an era shaped by giants, when my great-grandfather stood alongside legends like Dr. Martin Luther King Jr.

That wind carried me back to a moment I could only imagine, a time when even the smallest whisper of nature held the weight of an era. It was September 20, 1958. Dr. Martin Luther King Jr. sat in a bookstore, signing copies of his memoir *Stride Toward Freedom*, when he was critically wounded in a stabbing. The injury was so severe that doctors later told him if he had so much as sneezed, he could have died.

After two hours of emergency surgery, as Dr. King was being discharged from the hospital, my great-grandfather received a call from someone in King's camp. Dr. King was on his way to him.

The relationship between Reverend Dr. Ray and Dr. King was more than one of respect; it was a deep brotherhood. Dr. Ray and Martin Luther King Sr. first met as classmates at Morehouse, forging a bond so strong it naturally extended to the next generation. Their closeness left such an impression on a young Martin Luther King Jr. that he grew up believing Dr. Ray was his actual uncle, affectionately calling him "Uncle Sandy." It wasn't blood that bound them, but chosen family—a connection rooted in trust and love. Under Dr. Ray's leadership, Cornerstone Baptist Church became more than a house of worship.

It was a spiritual refuge and a beacon for those seeking strength in the fight for justice.

My foundation, my Great Grandpa Ray, was a man so grand that even in one of Dr. King's most trying moments, he carried him. He covered and protected those destined for greatness. He served as a spiritual anchor for a leader who changed the world.

And fortunately for me, he passed down that same strength, that same unshakable faith—the very essence of why I feel called to write this book: to explore the intersection of politics, purpose, and the humanity within it all.

As I watched through the window, I saw Great Grandpa Ray greet Dr. King with warmth and reverence. But just as I took in the moment, something unexpected happened. Great Grandpa Ray turned toward the window.

At first, I thought he was simply catching his reflection in the glass, but then his gaze deepened. It was as if he could see through the glass, through time itself—as if he saw me. My breath caught in my throat. I wanted to hide, to move, to do anything, but I was frozen in place.

He stared into the window, seemingly at himself, yet I knew the truth. It wasn't his own reflection he was seeing;

it was me. A knowing expression flickered across his face, as though he recognized me, as though he was silently telling me: I am with you.

Just as I took a step closer to be sure, my mom grabbed my arm, pulling me back to the present—the moment we had all been waiting for. The leaf slipped from my hands, and the vision faded. I snapped back to reality, standing once again on this crowded Brooklyn street. At just 4'5" at the time, already tall for my age, after being lost in the vision and absorbing every ounce of my great-grandfather's legacy, I suddenly felt so much smaller, so unaccomplished, so unaware of the vast world that existed beyond my childhood understanding.

As they prepared to unveil the street sign, a piece of my great-grandfather's legacy was about to be cemented into history: Reverend Dr. Sandy F. Ray Blvd. What I didn't know then was that, 25 years later, an honorable moment—one that would make me feel far greater than the small girl I was that day—would find its way to me.

A powerful politician, a man from this very neighborhood who had shattered barriers and redefined leadership, a man known for standing unwaveringly on the right side of justice, a man I would one day fall in love with, would look at me—Jasmine Ray—with great conviction, with a sincerity that resonated deep, and say words that would echo through time:

"Jas, your family lineage is that of a protector of kings, and you, too, were born for this moment—to stand in that same power."

Though I never got to meet my great-grandfather, I feel the weight of his prayers, the strength of his protection, and the undeniable pull of his spirit. That's the thing about ancestry: it reaches beyond bloodlines and into bone, into memory and instinct. His protector's nature didn't end with him. It lives within me.

Throughout my journey, I have felt something greater than myself—a force guiding me, an unseen hand shaping my path. A layer of blessings, a presence too powerful to explain but impossible to deny. A protector from the past, standing guard over a protector of the present.

And just as my great-grandfather was called to protect a King, I was called to stand beside one.

CHAPTER 1 - TWO YEARS

S ports have a way of bringing people together. Even if you don't understand the game, you can feel the electricity in the air. A stadium full of strangers becomes united by the thrill of watching teamwork and talent collide on the court. It's the perfect place to lose yourself in the moment, whether your team meets victory or defeat.

It was March 14, 2014. Playoff season. I was at the Barclays Center, watching the Nets take on the Spurs.

That night, I had the pleasure of sitting in the Red Bull suite. At the time, I was a Sports Consultant for Red Bull, a role I held for several years, working across events, athlete management, and video production. One of the standout projects I led was Red Bull Slaps, the brand's one-on-one street handball tournament—a bold initiative that showcased the raw talent, history, and culture of New York City's handball scene. Red Bull was in a phase of creative rebellion, pushing every limit in traditional and non-traditional sports marketing and diving headfirst into anything that lived on the edge, from skateboarding to snowboarding and everything in between.

My path to Red Bull wasn't traditional. In 2011, I brokered a deal between the company and an athlete friend of mine. As soon as we secured the deal—just when we should've been celebrating—he dropped me as his manager. I was confused but not surprised. I'd met betrayal before. So, in classic fashion, I pivoted. Instead of dwelling on the loss, I started advocating for myself, pushing Red Bull to let me help with their outreach efforts. The synergy was already there. I had built a name for myself in the sports world through the United States Wallball Association (USWA), a nonprofit I founded in honor of my late brother, Jonathan.

Sports weren't just something I worked in; they were in my blood. My father made sure of that. As a child, I was a softball player, occupying shortstop and hogging the MVP spot for years. I wasn't just playing—I was winning. Beyond that, I'm a fourth-degree black belt in karate and spent years as an instructor. Discipline, competition, and leadership weren't things I had to learn later in life. They had always been part of me.

When my brother passed—a star athlete in his own right—my perspective on sports shifted completely. I wanted to honor him, and the best way I knew how was by making an impact on kids his age: 15 to 18 years old. By then, I had already fallen in love with handball. Growing up in New York City, if you couldn't afford organized sports, you turned to the concrete courts, armed with that iconic blue ball you could grab for a dollar at any corner bodega, and walked away with hand calluses that would last a lifetime.

So I created USWA—not just to get kids into the sport, but to reach them where they were. It became bigger than the game. It was about mentorship, mental health, anti-bullying, and education. I built a movement, one that had 2,600 kids following us borough to borough, showing up for the game but leaving with something more.

Though I love sports, I have to make it clear that it's not for the sake of professional athletes. My mission was never about big contracts and endorsements. It was about community and the kids. I care more about what's happening at Rucker Park than the NBA. That's why my connection with Red Bull made sense—they weren't just sponsoring elite athletes; they were tapping into the raw, unfiltered essence of street sports. And that's where I thrived.

For a year, I stayed on Red Bull relentlessly. I followed up, pitched ideas, and made sure they knew my name. I wasn't just asking for an opportunity; I was proving I belonged in the room. Eventually, persistence paid off. They gave me a budget and a shot, tasking me with overseeing outreach for their upcoming handball tournament at Coney Island. I did what I do best: turned an event into a movement, packing the park with athletes, spectators, NYC street legends, and the raw talent who gave the game its relevance.

That night at the Barclays, I was feeling good. I was half-watching the game, half-soaking in the perks of being part of something bigger than me. Then, out of nowhere, the suite doors swung open.

A man walked in. He stood 5'8", wearing a crisp white button-down shirt, a brown Mr. Rogers sweater, and sporting the warmest smile I had ever seen. Behind him was a stampede of teenagers, all wide-eyed and restless. Within seconds, they rushed the food, filled the seats, and took over the space like they owned it.

I was stunned. The audacity was beyond me. Who are these kids? More importantly, why are they in my suite?

I moved toward the man who looked like he was supposed to be in charge, though from the way the kids were running the show, I wasn't so sure.

"Hey, how are you?" he said, extending a hand. "I'm Eric Adams, Brooklyn Borough President."

I introduced myself and shook his hand, but I also let out a laugh. Huh?

"What's a Brooklyn Borough President?" I asked.

Don't judge me. I swear, at that time, I had no idea boroughs even had presidents. It's funny to think that handshake was an unofficial portal into the political world I'd later step into.

I asked him what exactly a Borough President does, and just like that, a conversation unfolded. I told him about my work in sports, my role as a consultant, and the fact that I managed events and athletes.

He listened, nodding, intrigued. Then, he made a proposition.

"I'd love for you to collaborate with me," he said. "Let's do some work in Brooklyn."

We exchanged information, talked a little more, and then—like players leaving the court after a hard-fought game—we parted ways. But his energy stayed with me: the warmth of his smile and the quiet confidence he carried. Suddenly, I wasn't even mad anymore that they had hijacked my space.

The rest of the evening was cool. We watched the game, enjoyed the suite, and promised to stay in touch.

Looking back, the irony isn't lost on me. My heart, like that game, would soon find itself in a battle.

***

A few weeks later, I took Eric up on his offer to collaborate in Brooklyn. It was an ambitious idea, but I proposed building a temporary, portable handball wall at Borough Hall.

For context, handball is an extremely popular sport in Ireland, brought to America by Irish immigrants who inspired the Parks Department to build walls throughout the city. Today, you'll find a handball wall in nearly every NYC schoolyard and playground. But the sport carries a dual identity. While it's a staple of the city's parks, it's also often associated with the lower class and prison culture—sometimes dismissed as a "jail sport."

My vision was to challenge that perception by placing handball walls in unexpected locations: public landmarks and iconic spaces that demand attention. Borough Hall, with its steady foot traffic and prime location near The Plaza, felt like the perfect choice.

The idea was simple: let people experience the game in a different light. Picture professionals on their lunch breaks, pausing on the steps to watch a match unfold. A sport once overlooked, now commanding attention in one of Brooklyn's busiest corridors.

Eric's right hand, Ingrid, was instrumental in pulling together the blueprint. His team, already dismissing the idea, said the building's historical blueprints couldn't be found. But Ingrid found them and helped gather everything substantial I needed to present the idea.

As I sat in the intimidating conference room at Borough Hall, I felt the weight of the building's history all around me. The massive wooden doors, the oversized table that seemed to swallow the room, and the towering portraits of past leaders staring down—it was impossible to ignore the sense of power and permanence in that space, especially as I sat there with four of his staff members, all of us quietly waiting.

When Eric entered the room, the energy instantly shifted. The man I met at the Barclays—once guard down and easygoing—now stood taller, broader, and far more assertive. The meeting lasted about ten minutes. He loved the idea. He raved about how out-of-the-box it was and why it would be a great look for the organization. Before leaving, he instructed his team to figure out the next steps. I was thrilled.

As he walked out and the door slowly closed behind him, I quickly turned to the woman beside me and excitedly asked, "So what are the next steps?"

She flatly replied, "We ain't doing that."

I blinked. "What do you mean?"

"Building a wall at the plaza? No way."

I said, "But that's what the BP just said."

She shrugged. "The BP doesn't always get what the BP wants."

I was confused and completely taken aback. I went home that night, pacing back and forth in my kitchen. I was torn. Should I call Eric and tell him what happened the moment he walked out of the room? The nerve of them to put on one face in front of him and then change it seconds later. Was it really all just smoke and mirrors?

Would it be inappropriate if I called?

Eventually, I built up the courage and dialed his number. When he picked up, I immediately apologized for calling his cell. "I'm so sorry to bother you, BP." Then I got straight to it. I told him that while he was in the meeting, his staff had one tone, but the moment he left, everything changed. They completely flipped and told me it wasn't going to happen.

He laughed it off and thanked me for my honesty, then shifted the mood and changed the subject. I let out a silent sigh of relief, comforted by the warmth in his tone. We ended up talking for a bit—nothing too deep, just easy conversation.

Somewhere during that call, he offered me a job. After the call, I emailed him my resume but then politely declined the offer. At the time, I was in a good place, making good money, and truthfully, I didn't want to work for him—or anyone, for that matter.

Still, something shifted. That call opened a door. It was the beginning of a real line of communication and the start of our friendship.

CHAPTER 2 - TWO YEARS PART II

The next time we spoke, it was to take a walk. Every pair has their thing—whether it's discovering new restaurants or binge-watching a favorite series—every couple has that one ritual that's just theirs. Walking became ours.

It was our first time meeting as friends since that moment at Borough Hall. One night, Eric called and asked if I wanted to meet him at the Promenade in Brooklyn Heights.

It was a clear spring night, the kind where the air is crisp but gentle and the city feels calm, like it's finally exhaling. The Promenade is usually noisy, not only because of the residents and visitors but also because of the BQE, an old highway running directly beneath our feet. It's an aging artery hugging Brooklyn's western edge, pulsing with the rumble of heavy trucks and traffic along the waterfront.

He started asking me a series of deep, engaging questions, each one more thought-provoking than the last. Then he asked, "What do you think the purpose of life is? Why do you think we're here?"

I blurted out the first thing that came to mind: "To pro-create."

He stopped dead in his tracks, stunned. He stared at me like I had read his mind, then shouted, "What?!"

For a second, I worried I'd said the wrong thing. But his reaction wasn't disagreement; it was alignment. That was exactly how he felt, too.

If there was ever a moment when he felt relieved that my beauty wasn't just skin deep, that was it.

Just like the highway below us, overlooked, overburdened, but essential, our conversation turned inward, uncovering the unseen things that carry us, hold us up, and keep us moving.

***

After that walk, for two years straight, Eric and I began showing up for each other in all the small and big ways that mattered. He was my plus one when I was honored by the National Conference of Puerto Rican Women for my work in youth sports, and I showed up for him just the same. His team didn't ask questions—they knew who I was. The barriers moved before I even got there: no signing the book at Borough Hall, no walking through the metal detector, no announcing my arrival.

I'd run up the marble staircase leading to his office, just like I used to run down the carpeted aisle at Cornerstone as a little girl. Except this time, it wasn't a red carpet; it was cool marble beneath my feet, and I wasn't eight anymore. I never slowed down. They'd see me coming and simply say, "Hey Jas, yes, he's in his office," as I breezed past. I didn't even knock; I just walked right in. In those moments, I felt like my younger self again—free and completely at home.

It was more than a bond; it was an unspoken connection, the kind that transcends space and time. It felt like a spark we never saw coming, yet one that could never be undone.

We had a few spots we frequented, and Woodland on Fulton Street in Brooklyn was one of them. We'd go there about three times a week, always sitting in the same seat tucked away in the balcony area. One night, over a dinner filled with our usual mix of laughter and deep conversation, he mentioned he had to head downstairs for a meeting and asked if I wanted to join him.

Beneath the dining area was a cellar with a private room. When we walked in, I noticed a New York State Senator who happened to be a woman, which stood out in that environment, along with a future Assembly member and two union representatives already seated. The union reps caught my eye first. They were White, almost bald, and in great shape, their muscular builds covered in casual clothes with tattoos running up their arms. They didn't fit the image I had in mind of what a union rep might look like, and I wouldn't realize who they were until later.

I remember feeling uncomfortable—not because of the scene, but because of the small black dress I was wearing, which was tight and revealing. The fabric clung to my skin in a way that suddenly felt inappropriate. I tugged at the hem and folded my arms, hoping to make myself smaller. Embarrassment crept over me as I worried I looked underdressed. I slid into a seat slightly to the side, far enough to stay out of the meeting but close enough to listen in.

The conversation started calmly and cordially. I wasn't quite sure what it was about at first, until the union rep raised his voice and said, "They're not certified for OSHA. How can we get them jobs if they don't even want to take the test?"

That's when it clicked.

Eric came to that meeting with intention. He was there to apply pressure, and he made that clear. He threatened to challenge the construction of a high-rise building in Brooklyn unless the union hired more minorities. He was serious, he was frustrated, and he wasn't backing down.

"I intend to challenge it unless you've got a certain number of Black and Brown people working on that site," he said firmly. "You're saying they aren't certified, but are you posting flyers? Are you making phone calls? What kind of outreach are you doing? Because until I see diversity on that job, you are not, under any circumstances, breaking ground on that building."

The conversation got so heated that he rolled up his sleeves. The female senator, wrapped tightly in her shawl, tried to diffuse the tension and said softly, "Gentlemen, calm down."

But the moment had already escalated.

It ended combatively, with a final warning from Eric: "Try me."

You know that point in a budding relationship when it finally registers: this might be the one? That was the moment for me.

My heart burst with admiration. I had just witnessed the passion he had for his people, the courage it took to represent the underrepresented, and the qualities that make a real leader. There was no audience, just me. No cameras, no press, no performance—just a man standing fully in his purpose.

His heart beat for the men and women who were out of work and needed a chance. In real time, I saw the weight he carried and the mission he had accepted.

I was convinced. Not just of his passion, but of his purpose. Of the kind of man he was when no one else was watching.

***

It's rare for the public to truly humanize politicians, to see them as anything more than their titles and soundbites. That's precisely why they can be torn apart without hesitation, given no grace to falter, no space to be anything less than perfect.

But behind the podium and the headlines, they're just people—imperfect, curious, and craving connection like anyone else. I saw that firsthand one summer night when Eric asked if I wanted to join him at a friend's grand opening for a new hotel. By then, we had a full-blown friendship, and I accompanied him almost everywhere. We pulled up to a sleek, modern building glowing under a wash of blue fluorescent light.

To my surprise, the hotel was completely empty, with no red carpet in sight. I had imagined an eventful grand opening with all the bells and whistles, but instead, it was silent. Impressively, he had the key to this brand-new establishment. He opened the door and led me inside, through the echoing halls of a space that would soon be filled with people.

He showed me to a room, and my mind immediately went left. I wasted no time making one thing clear: I was not sleeping with him.

"I just wanna sleep," he said simply.

"Okay," I replied, though part of me wasn't sure if he was telling the truth. I nervously paced the room, picking up little knick-knacks like the small lotions they typically leave for guests. I peered out the window, trying not to be awkward.

Minutes later, I laid down. He did too—fully clothed, not a belt undone. He placed his head on my chest and instantly passed out. And somehow, in the quiet of that room, fully clothed, it was one of the most intimate experiences of my life.

I lay there, still, listening to his steady breathing, and thought to myself that this man is all alone. He's just looking for a safe space. And in that moment, I felt both honored and committed to the trust we had built and to holding that space for him.

***

Trust, for Eric, wasn't loud. It didn't need to be. It showed up in small declarations that carried real significance.

It was always clear what I meant to Eric, and what he meant to me. And if I ever doubted it, he confirmed it through his actions. I remember one moment in particular at a Turkish restaurant in Sheepshead Bay, when he told me I was listed as his emergency contact.

"If anything ever happens to me," he said, "everyone knows—to let Jasmine in the room."

He said it plainly, but with so much depth behind it. It wasn't just about protocol; it was about trust, about devotion. In that moment, I felt it—his quiet way of saying you matter to me more than most. It was simple, but deeply romantic.

And it wasn't just him who saw it.

The words I clung to weren't just "let Jasmine in;" they were "everybody knows." There was something about that phrase that stayed with me—something about being known, not in a loud or public way, but in the quiet, unspoken ways that mattered most. Being loved privately is one thing, but to have that love protected, that's something different. It wasn't about being the center of attention; it was about the quiet security of moving through his world with ease.

I could walk in and out of Borough Hall, slip into his office, know his passwords, visit his home in Bed-Stuy—never needing to say out loud that I mattered to him. And I preferred it that way. As someone naturally inclined to retreat from too much attention, I found comfort in the intimacy of his trust.

That kind of recognition doesn't always come in words; it reveals itself in the kinds of moments that stay with you.

We were lying on the grass in DUMBO on a beautiful spring day. The sun was shining, the skies were clear, and if you're from NYC, you know how the cherry blossoms bloom to life when the weather's just right. If you're not from here, days like that are enough to make you book a trip. People were stretched out on blankets, toddlers were running in the distance, and something about the moment just felt... magical.

We were planted, like we belonged there. In between Eric's meetings, we always found time to drift into something spontaneous, and that day, his driver waited nearby while we made a quiet pit stop in the grass. We lay there in our element, holding hands, our fingers laced together, when we noticed someone taking our picture.

We both glanced in his direction, yet remained relaxed. The photographer walked over gently and said, "Don't worry, I'm not getting your faces. I'm just photographing your hands. You two look so content."

To be seen as a reflection of happiness, even by a stranger, was enough to make me believe in the kind of love I could spend forever chasing.

***

I'd like to think the ways he'd let me in—not just into his space, but into his world, was unique to us. How trust, for him, looked like silence, like privacy, like choosing presence over pretense.

And then came the moment that would stand out above all the rest. In two years of friendship, and quiet gestures, nothing would come close to what happened that afternoon at Forno Rosso, a small restaurant on Flatbush Avenue in Brooklyn.

Just like with the hotel, Eric had asked if I wanted to attend a restaurant grand opening with him. I imagined a bustling scene filled with music, chatter, and people clinking glasses. But when we walked in, it was completely still. The restaurant was closed to the public. Every chair was flipped upside down and placed on top of the tables—except for one. Right in the center. A beautiful table, set just for us.

It felt like the climactic romantic peak of a film—the kind of scene where the soundtrack swells and time slows down.

I remember feeling impressed, yes, but more than that, I felt special. As we settled into the moment, I took him in. He wore beige khakis and a green polo shirt, his beautiful chocolate skin gleaming under the lights. He was deep in his workout era then, and the shirt clung to his chest and arms just enough to make me feel like I was developing a crush.

Before my time with Eric, there were very few moments in my life when I ever wanted to lean into my femininity. I grew up a tomboy—hair pulled back in a ponytail, black tights, sneakers on my feet, no makeup, no fuss. By this time, I was running a successful nonprofit dedicated to engaging youth through sports, and my focus had always been on impact, not appearance. But with Eric, something shifted. For the first time, it felt natural to put on a skirt, do my makeup, and move through the world with intention in the way I presented myself. With him, I felt an unfamiliar yet profound sense of safety—like it was okay to soften, to let myself be fully seen.

I've come to believe it takes a certain kind of man to inspire that surrender—not out of weakness, but out of trust. To make a woman feel so protected, so cherished, that she willingly embraces her softness, knowing it's safe to do so.

That afternoon, I wore a beige skirt and a black top that revealed a hint of midriff, my hair blown out straight. My eye makeup was dark and sultry. We were perfectly in sync, like we'd dressed not for the occasion, but for each other. The energy between us felt natural yet heightened, and we were suspended in it.

Then the chef walked over, his warm smile matched by confident hands. "What would you like to try?" he asked.

Eric handed him the menu without hesitation. "Make us your best dish," he said.

Then he turned to me, nodded with a smile, and said, "You don't know it yet, but you're going to be my wife."

I rolled my eyes and half-laughed. "Okay," I said, brushing it off, though I could feel the butterflies in my stomach.

"You'll catch up to that understanding one day," he replied.

It's funny—both times I thought I was walking into something grand and crowded, I was met with silence and intimacy instead.

And maybe that's the point.

For Eric, maybe grandeur wasn't performance; it was presence. It was the quiet, sacred decision to choose one person, one table, one moment, and let that be the entire world.

***

Moments like that told me more about him than any headline ever could. In the weeks that followed, we kept moving through life together. And then came the moments that were loud and full of chaos—like the night we went to J'ouvert.

I had on a bright orange dress, and my hair was curly. He wore a white T-shirt and khaki pants. We were headed out for an evening at a Caribbean festival.

Eric's calendar was a steady stream of invitations—from bar mitzvahs to political galas and everything in between—and I was there for many of them.

J'ouvert was a celebration known for its vibrant energy and cultural expression. The atmosphere was electric. Music pulsed through the space, half-dressed dancers moved with ease, and vivid costumes brought the scene to life with color and motion.

We were having a great time: taking pictures with the dancers, eating, laughing, and dancing. We were planted slightly behind the main stage when, out of nowhere, a bottle came flying through the air and smashed into a man's head right next to us.

Without hesitation, Eric grabbed me and pinned me between his back and the wall. The instinct was immediate—no pause, no panic, just protection. In that moment, I couldn't help but think: those were his cop instincts.

There was a quiet power in the way he moved, the way his first instinct was to shield me. It wasn't dramatic, nor was it performative—and that made it unforgettable.

I've never been someone who enjoys chaos, voluntary or otherwise. Rollercoasters were never my thing. More than anything, though, that moment was a reminder of what it meant to be connected to a man of stature. This wasn't just some random incident at a festival—it was a window into the turbulence that sometimes followed him.

In *Trials*, we go beneath the surface and into the heart of that world.

A full-blown riot had broken out on the rooftop of the Brooklyn Children's Museum. Bottles and fists were flying. When things calmed just enough to move, he grabbed my hand and pulled me out of there.

Police cars, ambulances, and sirens filled the air—an all-too-familiar soundtrack to a textbook New York City night.

Out of breath, we jumped into the car, looked at each other, and burst out laughing.

"Niggas," he said, shaking his head.

His comment wasn't solely about behavior. On the surface, yes, it reflected frustration with how some members of our community conduct themselves in certain spaces. But beneath that was something else.

Something historical.Something disappointing.

And we'll explore that further a few chapters down, in *Unapologetically Black*.

***

The beauty of what led to the shift in our story was patience. For fourteen months, there was no pressure to define what we were—no expectations, no demands. Just unspoken adoration, mutual respect, and something deeper simmering beneath the surface. That's the thing about bonds that solid—crossing the line feels almost sacred. There's a stillness before something becomes something more.

It was mid-2015, and without realizing it, we had entered a new chapter. Eric and I were headed to the Bronx Ball, an exclusive, upscale event held once a year. Dressed to the nines, we were ready for a glamorous night out. But by the time we arrived, the room had already settled, and everyone was seated. The plan was simple: walk in quietly and find our seats.

But plans rarely go as expected.

As we stepped inside, the Bronx Borough President was mid-speech in front of hundreds of guests. Then he paused, looked our way, and said into the mic, "And there goes my brother, Brooklyn Borough President Eric Adams."

Suddenly, a giant spotlight beamed down on us.

I almost died.

Eric grabbed my hand and whispered, "Don't let go. Keep walking."

That spotlight wasn't just a technical cue; it was a symbol. Because for the rest of the evening, without warning, without discussion, Eric introduced me to everyone as his lady.

Up until then, we hadn't put a title on anything. We never even discussed one; neither of us wanted that kind of pressure. Eric and I flowed so beautifully that it never came up. Yet butterflies swarmed in my stomach every time I heard him say it, as he said it to several people. I still wonder if it slipped out naturally or if it was a preconceived thought. Either way, it was a welcome change, though I wasn't quite sure if it would last.

For the rest of the evening, I watched him do what he does best: connect. Eric has this endless curiosity about people—who they are, what they do, what they've overcome. He loves to ask questions, and his interest is so genuine it feels almost childlike, untainted by agenda. Unlike many political figures, who are infamous for touch-and-go interactions and quick to dismiss those they don't deem valuable, Eric moves differently. He believes everyone serves a purpose and carries their own unique value. When he speaks to you, it feels like you're the only one in the room. That's how fully invested he is in the everyday person, and how undivided his attention is when he's getting to know someone.

I admired that.

He didn't just introduce me to folks; he promoted me. He told people to keep me on their radar, told them I was someone to know, someone to work with. He spoke my name and my accomplishments in every room, and I'll always remember how deeply I admired that.

After the event, we got in the car, laughing like kids. Somehow, we managed to get lost in our own city. If you're from New York, you know Orchard Beach at night is a maze—twisting roads, no lights, everything looking the same. It was pitch black, and we had no idea where we were. And if that wasn't enough, we ran out of gas, too. But instead of stressing, we just laughed harder. That was us—finding the fun in the unknown.

Eventually, we made our way back to his office. It was nearing midnight, and the city had quieted. The streets were empty of people, but not of movement. The low rumble of sanitation trucks echoed up Joralemon Street as they emptied the sidewalk bins one by one. Still riding the high from the night, we were giddy and light. When we settled inside, I leaned against his desk while he stood a few feet away, propped against the couch. Our eyes locked. There were no words.

Just a long pause. Just a silence so full, it felt like sound.

We stood there, smiling, caught in some eternal moment. The air between us was thick with everything we hadn't said—truths lingering for months, waiting for one of us to be brave enough to speak first.

And then, he moved.

He crossed the space between us with a look that said he already knew—that whatever came next, there was no turning back.

He didn't ask.

He didn't explain.

He just looked at me...

And in that look, I knew.

He had made up his mind.

He closed the distance like a man stepping into something he couldn't walk back from.

And then he said, "Fuck it."

***

After we crossed that line, the love and the fun only intensified. We were addicted to each other. The outings, the conversations, the deep dives into each other's minds—it all continued.

Eric was more than a lover and a friend; he was a teacher. He poured into me in ways I didn't even know I needed, introducing ideas that expanded my mind and shifted the way I saw the world. He recommended documentaries and books that left lasting imprints, like *You Are the Placebo* and *The Organized Mind*. He even introduced me to Gaia, a streaming platform for conscious living and spiritual growth. And when I told him I didn't have an account, he handed over his login and password without hesitation.

That was his nature—generous with his knowledge, eager to share what moved him. He would even create pamphlets for his staff, urging them to grow spiritually and intellectually. It mattered to him that those in his orbit were evolving. He didn't just want progress; he wanted transformation.

But even as I admired his vision, the Peter Principle often echoed in my mind. Eric refused to accept that some people had already risen to the limits of their competence. He believed so fully in the potential of others that he was determined to pull everyone forward with him. No one left behind. It was a noble conviction, almost sacred in its intent—but one that left him exposed. His loyalty often stretched too far, and more than once, it came at his own expense.

It wasn't until then that I realized I might be a sapiosexual, drawn deeply to the richness of someone's mind. There was something about the way he thought, the way he questioned everything, that made me lean in closer. Loving him felt like bliss. But getting to know the other sides of Eric—his relentless belief in people, his way of managing them—was something else entirely. It was fulfilling in the way true love often is: layered, imperfect, and challenging.

At times, I was frustrated by how blind his loyalty could make him. Yet even in those moments, it was clear: what made him difficult was also what made him extraordinary.

Over the course of our relationship, Eric never talk about his past struggles with dyslexia as a child. I learned later with the public that he always felt like "the dumb kid" growing up and carried the weight of that injustice well into adulthood. No matter what he accomplished, he still wrestled with a lingering sense of inadequacy. Yet, before I knew that particular struggle, I could see it in him—how hard it was to be seen as something he no longer believed about himself, but couldn't fully let go of either. Even as a grown man, there were moments when he reverted to that scared little boy in class, praying the teacher wouldn't call on him to read aloud.

He wasn't dumb; he was undiagnosed and misunder-stood.

And that feeling, of being overlooked, underestimated, even targeted, didn't end in childhood. It followed him into the NYPD, where speaking out made him a prob-lem, not a pioneer. And it stayed with him in adulthood, showing up in subtle ways. Sometimes that struggle took the shape of confidence; other times, it felt as if he moved through life with a quiet chip on his shoulder. As much as the world saw a man in power, I saw someone still fighting to believe he deserved it.

In that, I saw a reflection of myself.

I've lived with that same feeling of not being enough. I grew up in Sunset Park, a predominantly Hispanic neigh-borhood in Brooklyn. As a biracial girl, I was teased and singled out constantly. I had thick, coarse hair, and kids would call me "Brillo Queen."

My Aunt Rachel, whom we all affectionately called Titi Kelly, owned a hair salon on 4th Avenue and 48th Street. One day, through no fault of her own, she permed my beautiful Black hair, unknowingly altering the natural coils that made me who I was. Back then, no one really knew how to manage my thick, textured hair, so she was only doing what she thought would help.

I didn't think straight hair made me more attractive; I just never felt like I had a choice. My mother was strict, and in our house, obedience wasn't optional. When she told me to do something, I did it—no questions, no resistance. If you grew up with a Puerto Rican mother, you already know: her word was law, and defiance was met with a sharp "pow!" before you could even finish the thought. Speaking up wasn't an option because I already knew what the response would be.

Deep down, I started to resent being Hispanic, because in moments like that, my Blackness felt like an inconvenience.

To make things worse, my brother was a child model—featured in calendars and celebrated for being adorable—while I was the girl told to sit quietly on the sidelines at his photoshoots. It wasn't until we were both in our thirties that he unexpectedly apologized for the way I'd been treated as a child. He told me he'd known early on that something wasn't right and had carried the guilt into adulthood for never speaking up on my behalf. As he described it, he was "The Golden Child," and I was the one merely tolerated.

From early on, I was molded to be seen, not heard—to feel small. My voice was silenced, my talents dimmed. As a child, I played the piano, could hold a Mariah Carey note, and could mimic a Bob Ross painting from memory. But these gifts were never cultivated. The piano became "annoying," the singing was "too loud," and the painting was "too messy and expensive." That's when my anxiousness began to take root.

I started biting my nails until the raw skin on my fingertips showed—quiet cries for an outlet or for comfort. But instead of compassion, I was met with punishment. My mother carried a small pair of sharp scissors in her purse. Every time she went to cut my nails, if there were none to cut, she'd poke each of my fingers with the scissors, trying to force me out of the habit. But the habit didn't go away. The pain only deepened. Eventually, I grew numb to the sting of the scissors—and then, numb to everything. My heart hardened with resentment, not only toward my mother, but toward everyone who saw what was happening and said nothing.

Those were my earliest memories of praying to be strong.

It wasn't until I became a martial artist and joined a softball team that something inside me began to shift. I wasn't just good; I excelled. All the frustration, the silence, the years of feeling invisible finally had somewhere to go, somewhere to explode. Every punch, every swing of the bat, every sprint was a release. For the first time, I felt strong. I felt capable.

Sports gave me something my childhood never did: a place where I could be seen, where effort was rewarded, where my presence mattered. I wasn't too loud, too messy, or too much. I was powerful, and I was valuable.

That healing deepened when I moved in with my aunt and uncle. My Uncle Melo, already a black belt in Shotokan karate, had a sense of humor that could disarm anyone's seriousness. But he didn't tolerate foolishness. He believed in discipline and integrity. And my aunt, Titi Pilly... there's a special place in heaven for people like her. I entered their home broken, lost, and closed off. I barely spoke. But instead of pushing me to open up, my aunt wrote me letters, hoping her words would reach the parts of me too afraid and too angry to speak.

That gentle, patient, and non-intrusive strategy—combined with my uncle's structured, no-nonsense ways—slowly coaxed me out, like a snail emerging from its shell, cautious but desperate for warmth.

Growing up in New York City with an overworked mom stuck in survival mode meant there was little room for softness, for processing, for emotional safety. Life came at us fast. Between hardship, loss, and instability, there was no time to talk about it, let alone make sense of it. But sports gave me a space to feel it all. To release it. To move through it.

Whether it was the disappointment of a missed shot, the adrenaline of a sprint, or the raw confrontation of combat, sports became a metaphor for life itself. It mirrored the very real battles we face every day—just trying to survive and stay sane.

Looking back, I realize sports validated me. But for a long time, like Eric, I lived with the ache of not being enough. Those painful feelings don't just disappear, even when you "overcome" them. That invisible weight was the layer that bonded us. We were two kids who grew up feeling small, and that's where we found each other.

Our connection wasn't just about fun and games; it was about recognition. Even now, it feels almost impossible to put into words. I can recall the memories, the places, the conversations, but the feeling itself defies explanation. It was the kind of bond that felt rare, almost otherworldly—like something out of a storybook.

Whether we said it aloud or not, I think we were both trying to heal something. And that's what makes the moment I'm about to share so painful to recount.

One day in early 2016, Eric called and asked me to meet him at his office. I was excited to see him until I stepped inside. The moment I walked through that door, the energy shifted. I could feel it immediately: there was an elephant in the room, and it was waiting for me. I sat down, and he got straight to it. His hands were trembling, and he wouldn't meet my eyes. Then he said it: he couldn't see me anymore.

He didn't want to, but he had to cut me off. That's what he said. He couldn't function with me in his life anymore. Our relationship consumed his mind, and he needed space to pursue something bigger. He said he was onto something major—something he had to protect me from. He talked about feeling out of focus and undisciplined, always wondering what I was doing, where I was. It had simply become too much. The conversation was heavy and lasted for hours.

He was breaking up with me, and I felt my soul leave my body.

By then, I had learned to live with grief. But in that exact moment, I didn't fight for us. I didn't beg. I didn't show how much pain I was in behind that conversation. I just accepted his words, left his office, and shut myself off. It would be the last time I walked down that grand marble staircase. But this time, there was no security, no sound, no lights. Just me, in the dark, carrying the weight of that conversation back to my car, parked right outside Brooklyn Borough Hall. I prepared myself to block him out of my mind because it was the only way I could survive it.

How do you experience the greatest love and friendship of your life... and then survive the breakup?

I walked to my car and cried like a baby. Through the windshield, I looked up at his office almost hoping he would change his mind. The rain tapped softly against the glass, blurring the lights into streaks of color. Through the haze, I watched as the lights in his office flickered, then went dark, one by one. The sound of the rain and the weight of the moment made it feel like I couldn't breathe. In an instant, it felt like he flipped the switch on everything we had built. The light in my life... was gone.

CHAPTER 3 - WILLIE LYNCH

It has always fascinated me—the way Jewish communities have mastered the art of self-preservation. Their allegiance to one another isn't casual; it's intentional, generational, and deeply embedded in every layer of their society. They've constructed entire ecosystems designed to protect, sustain, and empower their people. From education to healthcare, transportation to finance, they operate within closed, tightly woven networks that prioritize collective well-being above all else. Their money circulates within their community, their institutions are built by and for their people, and their cultural pride is reflected not just in words, but in daily practice.

When I was organizing Wall Ball, I had a meeting with an NBA executive. I don't remember every detail of our conversation, but I recall saying something that must have lacked confidence, because he stopped me mid-sentence and reminded me: never be ashamed of doing things for your people, and always stand for your culture.

He then shared a story about David Stern, the former NBA commissioner, who was Jewish. He said that whenever Stern held meetings, he would end by asking, "Is this good for the Jews?" If the answer was no, they didn't move forward. Simple as that. And no one accused him of being discriminatory or prejudiced—because he wasn't. He was simply looking out for his people.

That level of dedication to one's own community—that unapologetic loyalty—is exactly what we, as Black people, are missing.

There's a word and cultural concept called *fargin*. It comes from the Yiddish language and speaks to what it truly means to belong to a community. When you're part of the Jewish community and you have a business, your people support you fully. If you misstep, they don't cancel you; they correct you. They help guide you back on course until you get it right.

Fargin is a practice that wholeheartedly celebrates achievement. It's a mindset that transcends competition and ego, embracing mutual support, accountability, and the hope in one another's success.

It's the kind of loyalty that sustains ecosystems—the kind of love we, as Black people, were systematically stripped of. And it's exactly the kind of practice we need to rebuild.

But I have to be honest: every time we've tried to build something lasting, we've been met with resistance. Not because we lacked the vision, but because the system feared our success.

It's historical and denying that history is part of the problem. Every time we, as a people, have attempted to create something of our own, we've been met with violence, sabotage, and systemic pushback.

We built Tulsa's Black Wall Street, and they bombed it.

We built Rosewood, and they burned it to the ground.

We marched, we protested, we organized in the movements of the 1960s, and they infiltrated, dismantled, criminalized, and killed our leaders.

Every spark of Black self-sufficiency has been extinguished before it could truly catch fire. But the deeper tragedy is what's been left behind. It's not just the external oppression—it's what's seeped into our psyche: the crab-in-a-barrel mentality, the distrust, the inability to see one another as allies instead of competitors. It's as if division was coded into us, passed down through generations like inherited trauma.

And to be honest, it's disheartening.

It's sickening.

And I'm fucking tired of it.

You've probably heard about the infamous Willie Lynch Letter. But let's be clear: it's not just a letter; it was a blueprint.

According to the alleged document, Willie Lynch, a British slave owner, was invited to Virginia in 1712 to teach American slaveholders how to control Black people for generations to come. His solution wasn't chains or whips; it was psychological warfare. His plan was simple: divide Black people, and you could control them forever.

His method was systematic and insidious. He instructed slave owners to break the Black man's spirit by emasculating him and stripping him of his power and his place within the family. At the same time, he urged them to elevate the Black woman—not to empower her, but to make survival her burden alone, conditioning her to raise her children in fear rather than in freedom.

He even broke it down into categories, instructing them to weaponize every difference: old versus young, light-skinned versus dark-skinned, male versus female, field slave versus house slave. He promised that if these divisions were nurtured carefully enough, they would last at least 300 years—long after the chains were removed and the whips laid down.

There's a long-standing debate about the authenticity of the Willie Lynch Letter. Some say it's a hoax; others argue there's no historical record of a man by that name. But whether the document is real or not, the plan it outlines has been undeniably deliberate.

And here's the truth: when you look around, it's not just visible; it's palpable. You don't just see it; you feel it.

Because make no mistake: whether widely known or not, a system was designed to break us, divide us, and turn us against one another so thoroughly that even without chains, we would still be bound.

We have inherited the very divisions described in that letter—whether fact or fabrication—with chilling precision. It lives in our communities, our politics, and our culture. We question each other's success and undermine each other's leadership. We emasculate our men publicly and call it accountability. We compete where we should collaborate. And we bury our unity under ego, trauma, and mistrust.

This isn't just historical trauma; it is living, breathing bondage. It is not a relic; it is an active playbook still running.

***

In late September 2024, the U.S. Attorney's Office for the Southern District of New York indicted Eric on federal charges. We'll get into those specifics in *Trials*, but as heavy as that reality is—and I don't say that lightly—the real betrayal wasn't the indictment itself. It was the reaction from within.

The Black community he advocated for, protected, and stood for was among the first to ridicule him, abandon him, and strip him of their support.

Understand the layer here: this isn't just about politics.

It's about conditioning.

It's about how deeply the programming runs. Somewhere along the line, we became a people quicker to tear down our own than to stand beside them. At some point, we learned to feel a twisted sense of relief—sometimes even joy—watching a Black man drown.

Not all of us, and not all the time. But enough for it to become embedded. Enough for it to feel instinctive.

And that—*that* is the legacy of a system designed to keep us fractured.

When Eric's White opponent, former Governor Andrew Cuomo, entered the mayoral race, the outpouring of love and support for him was overwhelming. He and a coalition of Black leaders gathered at Melba's in Harlem, arguably one of the most revered soul food restaurants in New York City, to champion him and pledge their support.

It's funny how politicians always seem to know exactly who to pose for. Race, class, culture—there are layers to it all, and even quieter divides tucked in between. Back in May 2025, at Cornerstone, I had a conversation with an elder who put it plainly:

"We're the educated, older crowd. He didn't go to Sylvia's; he went to Melba's."

Her point wasn't about food, and certainly no disrespect to Melba's. It was about signaling. How showing up in one space instead of another speaks volumes about who you want to be seen by, and who you're willing to be challenged by.

"We're a different class of Black," she added. "He won't be challenged in that room. But if he came to Sylvia's, we'd have real questions for him."

And yet, even among the handpicked crowd, this was the same Andrew Cuomo who resigned amid serious allegations: eleven women accused him of sexual harassment, and a federal investigation was launched into his administration's handling of nursing home deaths during the pandemic. More recently, he's faced scrutiny from the Justice Department over whether he misled Congress about his COVID response. Still, he remains a front-runner in the mayoral race—widely embraced by donors and political elites, praised in the press, and positioned as a comeback story.

So why is it that we can extend grace to him, but not to one of our own?

What makes it all ironic is that Cuomo's platform mirrors many of the same policies Eric once championed: aggressive policing, mental health reform, charter school support, and close ties to real estate interests.

So why is it that when Cuomo steps into the arena, he's met with solidarity and second chances, but when Eric does, the reaction is often skepticism and dismissal? This isn't about vilifying Cuomo—who, in many ways, has been a shrewd and effective political force—but about examining the selective grace we extend, especially when the accusations, policies, and optics are nearly identical.

What Eric is facing isn't unique; it's a pattern. Across the country, Black leaders are under siege—not just by their enemies, but by the very systems and communities that should be standing behind them.

In Chicago, Mayor Brandon Johnson has openly stated that racism still plays a central role in how he's attacked and undermined. In May 2025, the Department of Justice opened a civil rights investigation into his administration's hiring practices, citing remarks he made about appointing Black leadership to key positions. While his senior staff largely consists of policy-level appointees—positions typically exempt from Title VII constraints—the swiftness and tone of the DOJ's response speak volumes.

Critics rushed to frame his intention as discriminatory, yet the pattern is clear: when a Black man rises to power and dares to center his community, the backlash is immediate. The scrutiny comes from every side: internal and external, visible and invisible.

It's not paranoia; it's programming.

All of this only underscores a deeper truth: something is psychologically and fundamentally broken within our culture. Even the Chinese, who have endured their own share of oppression and exclusion, do not respond to adversity by turning against their own. No other race normalizes internal betrayal like we do. No other community has been so deeply conditioned to internalize violence—to view harm inflicted within our own neighborhoods as a moral failing, rather than as the result of systemic neglect, generational poverty, and intentional disinvestment.

And yet, we are the only ones expected to pretend it is normal.

What's happening to today's Black leaders isn't new; it's a story we've seen play out generation after generation.

David Dinkins, the city's first Black mayor, took office in 1990 during a time of intense racial tension and economic struggle. Despite his efforts, he was ousted after just one term. And as political strategist Hank Sheinkopf once put it, New York has a long tradition of scandal, corruption, and mismanagement across administrations — but the consequences have never fallen equally.

Bill de Blasio was accused of mishandling $2 billion in taxpayer dollars meant for mental health programs, and investigated by federal and state authorities for campaign finance violations. Rudy Giuliani's aides were pursued by prosecutors. Commissioners under Koch were arrested and indicted, with City Hall itself touched by scandal. Abraham Beame mismanaged the city into the 1975 fiscal crisis and was threatened with indictments that never came. Even going back nearly a century, Mayor Jimmy Walker's open ties to organized crime only brought action after years of scandal. Yet when the first Black mayor, Dinkins, presided over a period when crime rates were already trending downward, blame was laid squarely at his feet. The message is clear: it ain't the same for everyone. And Black leadership in particular, has always faced a harsher judgment, a narrower margin for error, and a swifter fall from grace.

Now, here we are again—with a Black man leading New York City—and history has already started the count-down.

I'm not saying Eric will suffer the same fate—there's still a window for change. By the time you read this, either he has defied the odds and secured a second term, or he's been pushed out like those before him. But as I write this, the narrative is already taking shape, and history feels danger-ously close to repeating itself.

In this city, it almost seems like Black mayors don't get two terms. David Dinkins didn't. And if we're not careful, Eric Adams won't either.

Why is that?

Why does power seem to come with a shorter leash when it's held by a Black man?

Why does the clock always run faster when the face at the helm looks like ours?

You'll see throughout this book that I am not excusing Eric's missteps. I'm naming his humanity. And I'm asking: where is the political humanity in return? Where is the *fargin*?

Instead of holding space for his flaws, working with him, standing beside him in the storm, many of the very people who should have supported him chose to tear him down.

Look at his administration. It is filled with Black and Brown people—Hispanics and African Americans who may never have had the opportunity to do what they are doing today if not for him. Eric brought everybody with him, and that deserves to be acknowledged and applauded. It's just as important to note that his team also includes White people, as well as individuals from every other race, culture, and religion under the sun. Why? Because that's what New York City is: a melting pot of diversity that should be reflected in any administration claiming to serve its people.

Yes, his administration has faced controversy and turbulence. And yes, as the head, he is responsible. But what strikes me most is this: no one gave him the chance to course-correct.

When Andrew Cuomo announced his political comeback, he said in a campaign commercial, "Did I make mistakes? Yes." And we took him back—quickly, loudly, and without hesitation. This isn't to say he didn't deserve it. In fact, I applaud his honesty and directness. That kind of accountability is rare, and it's a quality that makes a leader great.

However, it would have been powerful—restorative, even—to see that same grace extended to the man we elected. Because we didn't just believe in his campaign. We believed in his promise to change the face of New York City for us all.

And yet, when he stumbled, too many forgot that belief.

When will we stop demanding perfection from our own while extending grace to everyone else?

Because if we don't confront that truth, then yes, we are failing political humanity.

CHAPTER 4 - UNAPOLOGETICALLY BLACK

There has always been something undeniably powerful about melanated people — a brilliance, resilience, and capacity for creation that the architects of colonialism both feared and envied. It is precisely because of that power that centuries of systems were built to enslave, divide, and suppress us, to strip us of education and economic opportunity. Yet the very fact that so much effort was spent trying to contain us is proof of the magnitude of our light.

What we're witnessing today, through the crucifixion of Black leaders like Eric, is not just political backlash; it's spiritual warfare.

To truly understand what's happening right now, you have to look at the full arc: the betrayals, and the calculated steps that brought us to this moment.

Prior to 1936, most Black Americans voted Republican—the party of Lincoln and Emancipation. But the shift to the Democratic Party wasn't driven by shared values. It was economic. It was about survival. Roosevelt's New Deal offered jobs and relief to Black families during the Great Depression, even as his administration turned a blind eye to Southern segregationists.

By the 1960s, civil rights legislation under Lyndon B. Johnson—most notably the Civil Rights Act of 1964 and the Voting Rights Act of 1965—further cemented Black allegiance to the Democratic Party. But that loyalty came at a cost.

Johnson, fully aware of the political trade-off he'd engineered, reportedly said: "I'll have those n**rs voting Democratic for the next 200 years."

Though the quote's authenticity is disputed, its sentiment reflects a broader truth: Black political support was being courted not with respect, but with strategy.

That moment marked the beginning of a transactional alliance—one where our votes were expected, but our voices rarely respected. Black political power has seldom dictated Democratic policy. We became the party's foundation, its strongest and most reliable base—yet were too often treated like stepchildren.

In places like New York, the Democratic machine didn't just run politics; it controlled access. Power wasn't awarded for bold leadership, but for loyalty. Positions, resources, and influence were handed out based on how well you stayed in line, not how well you served your people.

Ironically, we're now witnessing another migration; this time, ideological. According to recent polling from Pew and Gallup, Black support for the Democratic Party has dropped nearly 20 points since 2020, especially among Black men. But this shift isn't because we've suddenly embraced conservatism; it's because we're tired. Tired of being used, ignored, and blamed.

Eric hasn't switched parties—at least not yet—but he's stepping outside their confines. And for that, they call him dangerous.

But what's truly dangerous is a system that only loves Black leaders when they're docile.

When Eric Adams co-founded 100 Blacks in Law Enforcement Who Care in 1995, it wasn't just an organization; it was a statement. A collective of active and retired Black officers took a stand against police brutality, racial profiling, and the injustices happening inside the very system they served. They raised their voices, risking their careers for truth, accountability, and the safety of the communities they came from.

Eric used his platform to expose injustice from within. And that kind of courage should've earned him protection from us, if from no one else.

But as always, when a Black man dares to disrupt the status quo, the backlash is swift and brutal. The NYPD surveilled Eric and his fellow members, treating them like threats instead of reformers. Rather than being celebrated for trying to heal a broken system from the inside out, they were punished—ostracized not just by the institution, but sometimes even by the very communities they were fighting for.

His story with that organization is just one chapter in a much bigger truth: the moment a Black man steps out of line, the full weight of the institution—and too often, the silence of his own people—comes crashing down on him.

Now, as mayor, Eric has been politically iced out, pressured to resign, vilified in the media, and boxed in by the same party he's spent his life trying to elevate. And his crime? Not corruption. Not scandal. Just disobedience.

When he criticized Joe Biden's handling of the migrant crisis and the financial toll it's taken on New York, he wasn't just breaking party lines; he was breaking protocol. And in politics, especially Democratic politics, that kind of deviation is dangerous. It's seen as crossing the line.

For Black leaders, it's damn near treason.

So when I hear someone like Andrea Stewart-Cousins—New York's first Black woman Senate Majority Leader—publicly call for his resignation, I don't just hear politics. I hear the sound of the machine demanding silence.

Let's be real: if Eric were White, or even a safer, more "polished" Black man, this would've been handled quietly, behind closed doors. But because he's unapologetically Black and refuses to follow the script, he's been publicly flayed. It's part of a long, painful legacy—a cycle we've seen play out across bloodlines and generations.

In 1949, my great-grandfather, Rev. Dr. Sandy F. Ray, stood alongside Jackie Robinson as they were summoned before the House Committee on Un-American Activities. Under federal scrutiny, they were forced to reaffirm their patriotism—to prove their loyalty to a country that still treated them as second-class citizens. Yet in that moment, they chose to speak truth to power, denouncing segregation and exposing the hypocrisy of a nation that preached democracy abroad while denying it at home.

Today, Eric stands in that same fire. The names have changed. The mechanisms have evolved. But the system remains. We're still standing before institutions that demand our loyalty while denying our humanity. Still fighting to be heard. Still pushing back against narratives designed to fracture, silence, and diminish us.

And now, we, Black Americans, must ask ourselves: Are we going to help fuel the fire, or stand beside those who dare to walk through it? Will we be complicit in the cycle, or will we finally disrupt it loudly, collectively, and unapologetically?

Let me be clear: accountability is not the enemy of solidarity. Supporting Black leadership does not mean silencing critique or excusing harm. Accountability must always remain at the center — for me as a citizen, for Eric as a mayor, and for all of us as a community.

But public execution disguised as critique isn't accountability; it's betrayal.

To every Black person who has turned on Eric: the system didn't need to take him down. You're doing it for them. When we destroy our own, we aren't dismantling oppression; we're carrying out its final step. What I am calling for is not blind loyalty, but a lowering of the temperature and a shift from destructive outrage to constructive critique. Our city deserves both truth and humanity in its politics.

Let me remind you of what Theodore Roosevelt once said:

"It is not the critic who counts; not the man who points out how the strong man stumbles, or where the doer of deeds could have done them better."

Eric is the one who dares to do. Who chooses to fight. Who stands alone in the arena. And what makes it even harder is that the ones surrounding that arena—pointing fingers, waiting for him to fall—are the ones who look just like him.

Roosevelt went on to say:

"The credit belongs to the man who is actually in the arena... who strives valiantly... who, at the worst, if he fails, at least fails while daring greatly, so that his place shall never be with those cold and timid souls who neither know victory nor defeat."

So while those who oppose him scoff from the sidelines and critique his every move, Eric remains what they're too afraid to become: a Black man bold enough to lead unapologetically.

This is what Eric meant at the Brooklyn Museum that night, when a fight broke out and he used the word "niggas" with disappointment. He wasn't just frustrated; he was heartbroken.

"That word isn't about people," he told me once. "It's about behavior. About forgetting who we are."

And many of us have. We've forgotten our assignment. Forgotten that we are the descendants of prophets, organizers, warriors, and truth-tellers—not political puppets or echo chambers.

Given everything we've endured, it's no surprise that many of us have been stripped of the tools to carry ourselves with clarity, confidence, or control. We were programmed that way. The dysfunction, the chaos, the self-destruction; it was planted in us, nurtured through generations of trauma, fear, division, and degradation. It wasn't born in us; it was bred into us.

So when we turn on each other—when we destroy our own spaces and sabotage our own leadership—we're not seeing ourselves. We're seeing the system's greatest victory. And the saddest part is, most of us don't even realize we're acting out the script they wrote for us centuries ago.

Eric Adams is in the arena. He is not perfect. But he is present. And he is ours.

If we are to be unapologetically Black, let it start here—with a refusal to help the world destroy one of our own just because he dared to lead.

We don't have to agree with every decision he makes. But if we can't stand by him when he's under fire, then we've learned nothing from the past we claim to honor.

Let us not forget: the system was designed to punish resistance and reward compliance.

That means when we see a Black man punished loudly, it's usually because he was doing something right.

And for that, we should not apologize.

We should stand.

CHAPTER 5 - TRIALS

It's been said that only the most broken people can become great leaders. Before stepping into the second-highest seat in America in 2022, Eric endured one of life's greatest losses: the death of his mother. Then, in 2025—after withstanding relentless public scrutiny, an indictment, and countless other trials—he lost his closest sibling, Sandra. These back-to-back heartbreaks didn't weaken him; they refined him. They shaped a leader forged in fire, one who governs with deeper empathy and unshakable resolve.

This kind of boldness—the courage to lead with both strength and vulnerability—is the bedrock of a politician worthy of office. The public gains nothing from leaders who tiptoe around hard truths just to preserve their careers. What a city needs, what a nation needs, are officials unafraid to speak reality aloud—even when that reality is inconvenient, even when it threatens their standing.

Eric chose that path.

The migrant crisis in America didn't just expose cracks in our immigration system; it revealed fractures within communities, ideologies, and even political parties. It became a test of identity and loyalty.

While most politicians defaulted to protecting their party—prioritizing optics and political capital over honesty—Eric made a different choice. He spoke directly to the crisis, placing the needs of New Yorkers above party allegiance, even when doing so came at a personal and political cost.

Immigrant communities themselves were torn between empathy and resentment, especially those who had followed the legal process. And for cities like New York, survival wasn't just political; it was logistical. Budgets were collapsing, shelters overflowing, and resources stretched to the brink.

But Eric didn't flinch. He walked straight into the fire.

As migrants poured across the southern border, sanctuary cities became landing zones that weren't backed by federal funding or a coherent federal strategy. This left Governors and mayors like Eric, holding the weight.

The conversation around immigration often pretends to be binary: you're either for open borders or against immigration altogether. But the truth, as always, lives in the gray. Eric didn't condemn migrants. He condemned a system that flooded his city with people, yet gave them no legal right to work, no infrastructure to thrive, and no funding to survive.

Between 2023 and 2024, Eric traveled to Washington ten times—quietly and respectfully—to meet with the Biden administration and ask for help. At first, he wasn't making noise or pointing fingers. He followed protocol, doing things the way his party expected: discreetly. For Democrats, "the right way" often meant staying quiet, waiting patiently, and protecting the administration's image, even as the cracks grew wider.

But instead of action, Eric was met with repeated dismissals. One official allegedly told him, verbatim, to "be a good Democrat." Another compared the migrant influx to a gallbladder stone, casually remarking, "It'll pass."

Eric knew better than to accept the brush-off. What was unfolding in New York wasn't just discomfort; it was dysfunction. His city wasn't being overwhelmed by people; it was being crushed by policy failure.

Still, he stayed in line and waited for change.

At the same time, a deeper theory was circulating—one Eric had heard but never publicly endorsed: that the Democratic Party was strategically keeping the border open, particularly under a Democratic presidency, with the long-term goal of naturalizing migrants, making them eligible to vote, and securing a loyal voting bloc. In cities like New York, where legislation was being pushed to allow non-citizens to vote in local elections, the theory didn't seem so far-fetched to those paying close attention.

But it was a contradiction. Migrants were being told they couldn't work, at least not legally. And yet, the same politicians advocating for their political participation offered no economic path forward. To Eric, it was insanity. His city was footing the bill for a federal failure. By law, he had to house them, feed them, clothe them. He was handed a humanitarian crisis with no tools and no support.

Eric's message was clear: no political future is worth sacrificing the survival of a city already pushed to its breaking point. This wasn't a rejection of immigration, but a demand for responsibility. Because when Washington turns away, cities like New York are left to carry the weight alone. And when he said that out loud, the silence from his own party was deafening.

Across the country, the debate wasn't just about immigration; it was about class. Many Hispanic Americans, especially those who had immigrated "the right way," through years of applications, fees, and pledges, viewed the influx with frustration. Some had even supported President Trump. Others, particularly in cities like Miami, stood firmly against illegal entry—not out of a lack of empathy, but because they remembered what it took to get here. To them, skipping the line is unfair.

This tension cut across racial lines, too. Italians, Haitians, Jamaicans—families who had come through the legal process—looked at the border crisis and saw chaos, not compassion.

Meanwhile, Republican Governor Greg Abbott of Texas decided he was done carrying the burden alone. As the border state absorbing the brunt of the migrant surge, Texas began bussing new arrivals to sanctuary cities across the country—including Denver, Chicago, Washington, D.C., and New York.

Critics called the move cruel and racially motivated. But Abbott insisted it was a wake-up call, not a racial tactic. He claimed he chose cities based on their sanctuary status—not the race of their mayors. That many of those mayors happened to be Black and were now left scrambling was, according to Abbott, nothing more than political optics.

What Abbott really wanted, he argued, was to show the rest of the country how unsustainable the immigration system had become.

And in that regard, he succeeded loudly.

***

As the buses kept coming and New York's budget buckled under the weight of emergency housing, healthcare, and food programs, Eric knew he wasn't alone. Other mayors were facing the same surge, the same strain, but they stayed quiet. Not by mistake, but by design.

In April 2024, at the African American Mayors Association's annual conference in Washington, D.C., Eric broke that silence. He didn't sugarcoat. He didn't sidestep.

He said what others were too afraid to: the federal government had abandoned them. The migrant crisis—unfunded, unstructured, and unsupported—was tearing through New York City. More specifically, Black mayors were being left to manage a national emergency with only local resources and no federal backup.

He called it a "planned disaster." He warned that ignoring the issue wouldn't make it go away and urged his fellow mayors to demand action. This wasn't a speech for applause; it was a warning, and a call for collective courage.

Eric wasn't grandstanding. He was trying to hold the door open for truth, for unity, for survival. But when no one stepped through it with him, he didn't step back.

Shortly after accepting that he was very much alone in this fight, Eric did what real leaders do: he stepped forward. He stood before cameras in New York City and said what most Democrats wouldn't dare:

"The President needs to close the border."

The moment made headlines and quick enemies. He had spoken out against his own party. Against the administration. Against the silence.

And not long after, the political consequences rolled in.

***

So is that what it comes down to? Speak the truth, and pay the price? Was Eric indicted because he broke the law or because he broke ranks with his own party and said what others were unwilling to?

By the time Donald Trump addressed a room full of elites at the annual Al Smith Dinner in October 2024, the indictment had already come down. Eric had been charged with accepting improper contributions allegedly made between 2016 and 2021—charges he publicly and vehemently denied.

In politics, accusations are often enough. The damage was done.

But then Trump did something no one expected. He broke from the usual political theater and stepped into a moment of eerie candor. Looking directly at Eric, he said:

"Mayor Adams, good luck with everything. They went after you. Nine months ago, I said, 'He just criticized the administration, he's going to be indicted.' Good luck with that. You're going to win."

The room, usually filled with polite laughter and the soft clink of wine glasses, let out a few nervous chuckles. But no one was truly laughing. What Trump had just said wasn't a joke. It was an undeniable truth, and it landed like a punch.

Trump's statement didn't exonerate Eric, but it reframed the moment. To many watching, it validated the idea that the case against Eric wasn't just about campaign finance violations; it was political punishment, plain and simple. A warning disguised as commentary, it delivered a clear message: don't speak out, don't break ranks, don't make noise, or consequences will follow.

The court case was still to come. But the narrative had already been set in stone—not only through court filings but also in public memory.

***

Memory is a selective storyteller. We forget the simplest things—what we had for lunch, where we parked the car—but when something life-changing happens, the details imprint themselves. We remember the clothes we wore, the scent in the air, even the exact setting on the thermostat.

In November 2022, I accepted the position of Director of Sports, Wellness, and Recreation in Eric's administration. Two years into that role, October 10, 2024, became one of those days memory refuses to release. I was in City Hall, leading a Wall Ball meeting that should've marked a moment of celebration. The room was filled with past leaders, athletes, and longtime colleagues. It felt like a full-circle moment—years of work culminating in one space, with one agenda and a shared purpose.

Wanting to make it even more meaningful, I sent Eric a text asking if he could come up and take a photo with the group. It was meant to be a quick, symbolic gesture. But what followed changed everything.

Eric stepped into the room like he always did—confident, composed, fully in command. He greeted everyone, posed for a quick photo, and shook a few hands. From the outside, it looked like business as usual. But then he looked at me, and everything shifted.

"Can I talk to you for a second?"

"Of course," I said.

We stepped into a room just outside the conference room, away from the crowd. The door closed slowly behind us, and the shift in his energy was immediate. No preamble. No cushion.

"You're on the radar," he said.

"Huh? Whose?" I asked.

"The feds," he said.

I immediately laughed out of confusion, maybe nervousness. I thought he was joking, being dramatic. But he wasn't. His voice didn't waver.

"They're monitoring everything and everyone," he said. "You're on a short list of people that have frequent contact with me. I just wanted to make you aware."

Then he excused himself, just like that.

I stood there frozen. Shocked. Confused. I didn't even know what to feel. I walked back into the meeting think-

ing, *What the hell just happened?* One minute, I was leading an exciting conversation, talking about something that
meant the world to me. The next, I was spiraling.

Everything they said blurred into background noise. Their
voices moved around me, but none of it landed. I couldn't
process a thing. My head was spinning.

They're coming? Radar? Feds?

I sat there, nodding like I was present, but I was somewhere else entirely. Everything felt off-axis, like I'd been
pulled into a different reality. And there was no going back.

This is how trials begin: not in a courtroom, but in a quiet,
unsettling moment when you realize you've been swept
into someone else's storm.

***

The next morning, I woke up disoriented. I kept replaying
the night in my head, trying to make sense of what had
happened. *Why me? Why now? Was I caught in something
I didn't even understand?*

The only person I trusted to guide me through a moment
like this was gone. My attorney and mentor, a relationship

I had cherished for fifteen years, had passed away on January 1st, that year. His wife, also a lawyer and someone I deeply respected, was the only person I could think to call. I didn't explain much over the phone. I just said, "Can I come see you?"

She lived in Princeton, New Jersey. I got in my car and drove the entire way in silence.

When I arrived, I told her everything I could: what I knew, what I felt, what had happened so far. For someone usually so full of opinions and certainty, she was suddenly a woman of very few words.

And that's when I knew it was serious.

She told me I needed to be careful. That I needed real protection and someone who specialized in cases like this. "I'm not the one to walk you through this," she said, "but I know someone who can."

Within hours, she connected me with a white-collar crime attorney at her firm. I gave him a quick overview by email, and within minutes, he told me to come in right away.

He was working remotely that day and suggested we meet near his home. I didn't hesitate. I got in my car and drove all the way to Westchester, in the middle of Friday traffic, because the fear in my chest was louder than anything else.

He later told me that my actions—the urgency, the transparency—probably saved me. "People who are guilty hide. People who are innocent panic."

We sat in a restaurant for hours, and I told him everything. He didn't sugarcoat anything in return.

"If you care about your freedom and your children, you need to get ahead of this now," he said.

My body went cold.

He said it again: "They're going to come to you. It's just a matter of time. It's better if you go to them first. Grace is only extended when you move before they do."

I sat there, holding back tears. I wasn't a criminal. I get mad when people litter. And I hadn't even been around Eric during the years mentioned in the indictment. Yet suddenly, my name and relationship were being pulled into something massive — a storm I hadn't created but was now forced to weather. It wasn't just the humiliation of being tied to allegations that didn't belong to me; it was the terror of realizing how quickly perception could shift, how fragile reputations were, and how little control I truly had once the government placed me under its microscope.

Chaos was erupting all around me. Friends and colleagues were being treated like criminals, stripped of their dignity as their lives were turned upside down. It was disheartening and terrifying, and I couldn't shake the fear that I might be next.

Winnie Greco, someone I consider a dear friend—Eric's longtime aide and liaison—had her home raided and ransacked. From what I read, she was handcuffed, humiliated, and pulled into the whirlwind surrounding the indictment. It shook me to my core.

Winnie wasn't just a name in the headlines. I first met her through Eric in 2015, when I was on a mission to manufacture my own handball. All the top brands were producing theirs in China. That year, I boarded a plane with nothing but faith, and Winnie made the experience unforgettable. She picked me up from the airport, settled me into my hotel, and that very night, invited me to a meeting that changed my life.

As luck would have it, I met Mr. Ding that evening—a powerful, wealthy economist in Shanghai. For the rest of the trip, I was treated like royalty. I carry those memories vividly: walking the Great Wall, visiting Beijing's ancient temples, falling in love with a culture that embraced me as one of their own. The trip wouldn't have been half as magical without Winnie. Her generosity and charm left a lasting impression.

Seeing her now—forced to resign, her name dragged through the mud—was devastating.

I left Westchester barely holding it together. I didn't go home. I didn't sleep. I couldn't even think clearly.

I called Benny, a sharp, brilliant Wall Street friend who'd had his own run-in with the feds years ago. If anyone could give me real advice without the fluff, it was him.

We met for breakfast the next morning. I was so scared I didn't even want my phone near the table. That's how shaken I was. I placed it on a separate table altogether.

When he sat down, I looked him in the eye and said, "I think I'm in trouble."

He listened carefully, nodded a few times, then said it straight:

"Jas, if I were you, I'd get ahead of it. You can either be on the government's good side or their bad side. But make no mistake, they're coming."

And there it was. The third confirmation I needed to be proactive.

I stared at my plate, hoping for some other sign. But deep down, I already knew he was right.

Later that day, my attorney called and told me the feds wanted to see me. I asked if he had given them my name. He said yes, but that they already knew who I was. That's when it hit me: Eric was right. I called my mom and told her to come get the kids. I was shaking, sweating, terrified. But I went in.

I had managed to stay under the radar for over a decade, and that level of privacy meant everything to me. If someone had snapped a photo, it could've been a disaster. So instead, they agreed to meet in an unmarked, obscure office near City Hall.

Before we went upstairs, my attorney met me in my car. "We don't have time for prep," he said. "You'll just have to trust me. The goal today is to sign a proffer and tell the truth before this goes any further."

I nodded, numb. I didn't know any better. There had been no prep, no plan—just a few whispered instructions in the car. Then I was led into a room with four federal agents.

I was greeted by Hagan Scotten. He was strangely kind. "Hi, Jasmine," he said. "Thanks for coming." His tone was pleasant but almost too pleasant.

I don't remember how long I was in that room. Time melted. Agents kept coming and going. At one point, they left with my attorney. Then came back. Then left again. When they returned, we signed the proffer agreement. I thought it meant I was protected. But then they explained, "We can't use anything you say here against you... but lying to a federal agent is a crime. So don't lie."

That's when it hit me: immunity wasn't something they could hand me in that room. Only the court could grant that. In that moment, I realized just how exposed I really was.

I didn't have anything to lie about. Honestly, I didn't even realize what I was saying mattered.

They asked me about my relationship with Eric, my background, and where I grew up. I said Brooklyn and Staten

Island. Without missing a beat, they replied, "Didn't you also live in North Carolina?"

They knew everything.

The whole thing didn't feel like an interview. It felt like a confirmation.

And then came the moment.

My attorney, the same one who claimed to be protecting me, turned and said, "Jas, show them what you showed me."

I stared at him, thinking, *What the fuck? What happened to attorney-client privilege?*

They asked me to unlock my phone, and I did. The lead prosecutor leaned in, clearly troubled by the spelling of a word he'd seen. He squinted at the screen, trying to sound it out.

"Yeeer? Yerr?" he said, confused.

He looked at me, eyebrows raised, eyes narrowed, then glanced at his colleagues. "What is this? What does this word mean?"

They passed my phone around like it held national secrets—completely puzzled, trying to crack the slang.

I laughed. "It's 'Yerr.' It's a term of endearment we use, you know, in the hood. It means 'what's up,' just a greeting."

They half-believed me, still eyeing the phone like it meant something way deeper than it did.

The cultural disconnect didn't just fill the space; it built the room, painted the walls, and locked the door behind us.

After we got past that, they continued scrolling, found the message, and flipped the screen around. I still don't remember what that message said. But whatever it was, they looked at each other and said, "Mm-hmm." They didn't take my phone. They just nodded, like they'd found exactly what they were looking for.

I closed my phone. And something inside me closed with it.

Then they asked to speak with my attorney again; this time, outside. They left me sitting there alone for over twenty minutes. When they finally returned, it was like they had just cracked the case wide open, and I had no idea what the hell had just happened.

We walked back to the elevators and rode down in complete silence. Outside, my attorney finally turned to me, excited like he'd just hit the career jackpot, and said:

"This is the Super Bowl of all trials. And you're the star witness."

I looked at him, stunned by the words coming out of his mouth. What the fuck just happened? How? What am I missing?

Then he said it: whatever they saw had confirmed something for them. And now, I was being considered a key witness in a superseding indictment.

I was truly puzzled and felt sold out by my own lawyer. It was becoming painfully clear that I hadn't just walked into that room; it felt as though I had been handed over.

***

That night, I went home and cried. I couldn't wrap my head around how I'd become the key witness in something I barely understood. I called Eric to tell him I'd just been interrogated by the feds. He froze.

"I'm not allowed to talk to you," he said.

And for the first time in ten years, something between us felt broken. The breakup was one thing. But this? This felt like betrayal. Maybe he was angry at me; I don't know. But I do know I was furious with him. He'd left me with nothing but a vague warning about being on their radar and no real preparation for the storm that followed. It felt like abandonment.

Later that day, I got a call from a mutual friend who didn't waste a second blaming me.

"You need a real attorney," he snapped. "Why'd you even go in there without proper counsel?"

He was yelling, and that's when I snapped back.

"Where the hell were all of you? Why didn't *you* get me an attorney? How was I supposed to react?"

In hindsight, I can't even regret finding counsel on my own. Because that day at the Wall Ball meeting, all Eric gave me was a warning. He didn't give me an attorney. He didn't offer any guidance.

After that phone call, the real search began. I called twelve attorneys in one day. Half of them had conflicts; they were already representing someone else tied to the indictment. It felt like emotional entrapment.

By lawyer six, I smartened up. I started leading with:

"Before I say a word, do you have a conflict that would prevent you from representing me?"

Finally, I called Chuck, a trusted friend and attorney. I told him I'd just landed in some shit and needed someone who could pull me out of it.

Chuck sent me to Jason Foy, a Harvard-educated, brilliant, no-nonsense lawyer. And the moment I met him, I knew he was the one. I wasted no time terminating the other attorney.

Jason was tough—sometimes even mean. He referred to Eric as "ya boy," challenged me on my political views, and even joked that we might as well be playing for the other team, especially with rumors swirling that Trump was considering bailing Eric out. He wasn't letting that slide.

But he promised me one thing: "I'm going to get you out of this. But you have to listen to me."

And I did.

When I told Jason everything that had happened, he was furious.

"He did *what*?" he said. "You've got to be fucking kidding me."

From that day forward, Jason took control. And when the subpoenas started—October, November, December, January—he went to war for me every time. Every knock at the door, every email, every call felt like another battle, but this time, I wasn't fighting alone. This time, I felt protected.

From October 2024 to March 2025, my life was hell. I was subpoenaed four times, interrogated repeatedly, and gained 20 pounds from the stress. Sleepless nights bled into endless days. My world shifted overnight: from handball courts to courtrooms, from purpose to pure survival. I still don't fully understand how anything I said could be useful to them. At one point, things were so intense you'd think I was Keyser Söze.

After my second appearance before the grand jury, I got a call from the *New York Times*. The writer seemed to know everything—my testimony, my involvement—and just wanted me to confirm it was really me. When I answered the phone, they were polite at first. "I know you recently testified in the Eric Adams indictment." I played dumb, pretending not to know what she was talking about. But she pushed: "Well, we know it was you. If you don't want to talk to us, you can just give us the name of your attorney." I replied, "Why would I have an attorney?"

It was hard to lie like that, especially when I'd always prided myself on telling the truth. For the first time, I felt guilty.

Then came the deeper betrayal. A high-ranking member of the administration—a woman I admired, someone I believed had Eric's best interests at heart—went to the government and claimed I hadn't been completely truthful. It hit me like a punch I never saw coming. She was a woman of color, a mother, someone I thought understood the stakes. And yet, she'd turned me into a scapegoat.

Next thing I knew, Jason called me. But this time, he wasn't on my side.

"I thought I told you not to talk to anyone about this. Did you speak to someone at your job? Now you're putting yourself in harm's way. And if you land in jail, you'll have no one to blame but yourself."

I cried again—not because he was angry, but because the thought of being separated from my children was too unbearable to process.

And then came another subpoena.

By this time, I thought I knew what to expect. But I wasn't prepared for what came next. This time, I wasn't treated like a witness. I was treated like a suspect.

The DOJ's tone had shifted. There was no more courtesy, no more patience. Every question felt like a trap. Every silence felt like a verdict. And, every look felt like suspicion. That's when it hit me: I was no longer just part of someone else's storm; I was standing in the eye of it.

***

Days later, CBS News showed up at my front door. I wasn't home, but my friend was. He called me, panicked, saying the press was outside asking questions.

Later that day, the CBS reporter called my cell directly. He got straight to it—no courtesy, no buildup. He said he knew about the relationship between Eric and me and threatened to expose it. It wasn't just invasive. It felt deliberate. Like he wanted to rattle me, and it was working.

I tried to reason with him, to stay composed, but I broke. I told him I was a mother, that I'd been working in public service for over a decade. I had given everything to this city, and now I was being dragged into something I barely understood. I was screaming for some compassion.

To my surprise, he softened. He told me our conversation reminded him of something his wife always asked: why couldn't he just write a positive story?

"I did my research," he said. "I know all you've done for this city, and in the name of your brother. You're the kind of person who should be serving in government. But I have a boss, and I was told I had to write this story. I'll leave out what I can."

And he did.

The final piece wasn't about the indictment, the testimony, or my personal relationships. It focused on a conflict-of-interest waiver—a routine form I had filed to lay out the parameters of managing parts of my daycare while working in city government. That was it. No scandal. No smear campaign.

When I read it, I cried again; this time, from relief. I even sent him a text to say thank you. "I understand you have a job to do...you could've been aggressive, but you were fair, and I appreciate that."

He replied, "Jasmine, I want to thank you for saying that. It actually means a lot to me. In stories like this one, I always struggle with balancing the public's interest with the fact that public servants (who are the subject of the stories) are human beings too – with careers and lives that aren't black and white."

That moment didn't undo the fear or chaos of it all, but it reminded me that even in the ugliest moments, someone somewhere might still choose to be decent and humane.

***

I know some of you may be wondering why I handled things the way I did in the beginning. The truth is, I didn't fully trust Eric at the time. Between 2016 and that moment, too many questions had gone unanswered. And once again, I found myself alone—left to interpret the weight of the moment without him, without my attorney, and terrified.

I've always respected authority. I was practically raised by cops. And while I never intended to compromise Eric, you know that saying, "The truth will set you free?" My response to the federal investigation came from a girl shaped by years of conditioning—someone who grew up believing in law, order, and doing what's right.

That respect for structure and discipline was deeply influenced by a man who embodied both: John Maniel, aka John the Cop.

There are people so uniquely special that they almost seem out of their minds.

John the Cop was exactly that—an NYPD officer with a deep love for karate. His legend wasn't built in a precinct or written into policy. It was forged in sweat, discipline, and a makeshift dojo tucked inside a Brooklyn garage.

Known as "Karate Cop" or Shidoshi, meaning Grand Master, John was a force: bold, courageous, and unapologetically daring. He challenged every so-called tough guy to put down their weapons and fight like a man. And they did. Because if you were lucky or troubled enough to encounter him, you didn't leave the same.

Who else do you know who would walk into gang territory and ask the hardest person on the block if they were man enough to learn how to fight? That was John.

There was a woman in Brooklyn who owned a residential building overrun by gang members. She hired Shidoshi to help. Most people would've called the cops. Instead, he brought his black belts. They didn't come in with guns, but with bats and gloves, and challenged the gang members to fight. That day, and on many others, he did a clean sweep.

From that moment forward, those same men became a positive force in the community. Under his discipline, they learned more than survival. This was the 1980s, when crime was rampant and opportunities for young Hispanic males were few. Many of them went on to earn black belts, then became law enforcement officers, youth mentors, and men and women who gave back to the city that raised them.

But Shidoshi didn't stop with the streets. He swept through the system, too. Officers from the Department of Investigation, Port Authority, Department of Corrections, and NYPD all came through his dojo, drawn in by his mentorship, guidance, and tough love. I remember being a young girl, watching them walk in still in uniform—only to change clothes and step onto the mat like everybody else.

***

I was around 13 when my parents divorced, and everything in my world shifted. My mom bought a house in Stapleton, Staten Island, with her now-husband, Raul. Not quite ready to ease into that new living situation, I moved in with my aunt and uncle instead.

My uncle didn't believe in gray areas: just right, wrong, and discipline. Within days, he gave me an ultimatum: "If you're going to live here, you're going to the dojo." There was no debate. No compromise. I didn't have a choice. So, dojo it was.

Like so many others, my uncle had been pulled off the streets by John the Cop. He'd lost his mother young, his father wasn't around, and the streets became his compass. But Shidoshi found him, pulled him in, and changed the course of his life. He didn't just teach him how to fight; he taught him how to live with integrity and discipline. And my uncle brought that same discipline into our home.

One thing I know for sure: my uncle was hard on me. Relentless, even. It felt like I was always singled out for the toughest ride. Whether it was workouts, sparring, or everyday discipline, I had to give more of myself just to be considered decent. And to be honest, I was always up for the task. I'd be damned if the highest-ranking Black belt in our school had a weak niece. So I accepted every challenge.

He never put me up against girls either; I always had to spar with male counterparts. Every moment felt like a test, and every test, a battle.

Looking back, I get it now. The pressure and the high expectations weren't punishment, but preparation.

Tio Melo, if you're reading this, thank you. You didn't just train me. You toughened me up for a world that doesn't go easy on girls like me.

Shidoshi was a New York City police officer, but more than that, he was a warrior with a vision. He believed in reaching at-risk youth through unconventional methods—long before it was fashionable or backed by formal programs.

Today, someone would probably sue if you invited them to a fight and then kicked their ass. That's just the world we live in now. But back then? Men were cut from a different cloth. Walking away with a black eye, a busted lip, or a twisted ankle wasn't grounds for a lawsuit; it was a rite of passage. Those bruises weren't shameful; they were the mark of strength.

Shidoshi created a ripple effect that spanned generations. The troubled young men he pulled off the streets in the '70s and '80s grew into community leaders—many serving the city for decades, some still in uniform, others just now approaching retirement. And here I am, serving in a mayoral administration, carrying the weight of those same lessons. The city is better for it, and so am I.

Over time, Shidoshi built a Federation, planting schools in Brooklyn, Maryland, and California. My uncle eventually opened his own dojo under that Federation: Sunset Park Martial Arts (SPMA).

I earned my Black belt under my Uncle, who had earned his under Shidoshi. Their discipline, fearlessness, and unwavering sense of purpose are etched into my DNA. Shidoshi passed away in March 2025, but his legacy lives on—moving through generations, carried by each of us he trained, pushed, and believed in.

Because when someone teaches you not just how to fight, but how to live, how to lead, and how to carry yourself with honor, you don't forget. You pass it on.

***

Just as you're reading these words now, I challenge you to imagine sitting across from me, watching my every move as I jog through a park. To your right, you see a harmless kid in a jogging set and hoodie—just out enjoying the day. But now, glance back at me. Do you notice the sudden sweat forming on my face? The hard swallow down my throat? Maybe that's too subtle. Maybe what you'll really notice is my pace shift—the way my route suddenly veers off course.

That's because I don't see a harmless kid anymore. I see a short police officer in a hoodie, ready to stop me mid-run and lock me up.

Tell me, do my mannerisms look strange to you?

Anxiety has been living in my body since the day Eric told me I was on the radar. And it's taken a toll on my mind, on my peace, and on my everything.

In April of 2025, I was in my office on the phone with my dad when my heart suddenly started racing—five times faster than normal. The windows in my office were frosted glass, but I could still make out the shadows of four men in suits heading toward me. The sound of my heartbeat drowned out my father's voice. My body shook like an earthquake had hit. It felt like my heart was about to leap out of my chest.

The door opened. The men walked in, smiling warmly. One of them extended his hand and said, "Hey, I'm Kaz, the new deputy mayor. Just wanted to introduce myself."

Relieved but fighting back tears, I abruptly hung up the phone and broke down crying. It was only 10 a.m., the workday had just begun, but I packed up and left the office without looking back. I called my mom, made arrangements for the kids, and by the next day, I was on a flight to my grandmother's house in Carolina, Puerto Rico.

I needed my safe haven. I needed peace. I needed to breathe again.

***

In life, we all go through trials. Eric, the man at the heart of this story, has faced his share. In this chapter alone, you've met people like my Uncle Melo, shaped by adversity, and Shidoshi, who turned hardship into discipline. Even President Trump, no matter how you feel about him, has walked through fire in full view of the world.

Hardship doesn't care about titles, personalities, race or public perception. It strips us down to our most human selves.

For me, from the moment I took my first breath, life has been a series of trials and tribulations. Maybe you've already faced your own. Or maybe you're standing in the thick of one right now. Because the truth is, none of us is immune to life's weight. Pain has a way of humbling us all.

But there's something that makes that weight easier to carry: People. Grace. Compassion.

The kind of quiet strength that shows up in the form of a friend, a teacher, a stranger who listens or a moment of clarity that reminds us we're not alone.

No one makes it through unscathed. But if we're lucky, we make it through bruised, not broken.

That's the goal—not perfection, but survival, with dignity intact.

After months of chaos, scrutiny, and silence, the dust finally settled:The case against Eric was dismissed in May 2025, with prejudice.

The indictment may have bruised Eric's reputation, but in the end, it unraveled under the weight of its own political performance. In March 2025, the *New York Post* published internal emails from Assistant U.S. Attorney Celia V. Cohen, who admitted that "we did a lot of gymnastics around the influence point" — a striking acknowledgment that prosecutors stretched the bounds of law in an attempt to make the charges stick. That phrase — "legal gymnastics" — now stands as a symbol of how fragile justice becomes when politics takes the lead. Yes, some of Eric's choices were tacky — airline upgrades and the like — but they never amounted to criminal behavior. Any credible legal expert would agree on that point.

What this case revealed was not just the hunger for scandal in our political system, but how easily that hunger overlooks the people behind the headlines — the families, staffers, and communities whose lives are shaken by each allegation, each subpoena. It's easy to play chess with other people's lives when you don't see the board from their side. But perhaps that's where the lesson lies — in choosing compassion and humanity over headlines.

Although it might be wishful thinking, that, ultimately, is what *Political Humanity* seeks to confront — the cost of power, the collateral of ambition, and the urgent need to put people back at the center of the political narrative.

I'm writing this chapter and this book not to rewrite the past, but to reclaim it. To tell my truth, in my voice.

Whether you walk away with judgment or empathy, admiration or skepticism, I can live with that.

Because for the first time, this story is mine — and no one else gets to define it.

CHAPTER 6 - THE CALL

No matter your spiritual beliefs, some moments feel meant to be. Life unfolds through a chain of people and places: a friend's invitation that leads you to the person you'll marry, a phone call that connects you to the partner who changes your life. I don't see these as accidents; I see them as openings. What comes next is on us. Our choices, for better or worse, either move us closer to purpose or lead us off course. When you understand this and hold a deep respect for God's plan, there's comfort. What's meant for you won't pass you by, as long as you're willing to do your part.

Destiny doesn't force its way into your life. It whispers. At first, the nudge is soft and subtle. But if you ignore it, the whisper becomes a knock. Ignore the knock, and it can feel like the universe is throwing a brick through your window. Keep ignoring it, and eventually, it walks away, leaving you to chart a different path.

I see life as a game with levels to unlock. The signs are always there. I believe it's on me to notice them and rise to the occasion. I've learned that potential isn't what's missing; action is. Too often, we ignore the signals, or we see them and fail to move accordingly.

2017

I always knew the legacy in my last name, but I wasn't fully conscious of its weight. My great-grandfather, Reverend Dr. Sandy F. Ray, was a force in his own right. Yet I carved my own path, separate from what he built, until destiny's time arrived.

One day, my fiancé at the time, Matthew ("Matt"), and I found ourselves in Bedford-Stuyvesant. Matt, a skilled videographer rarely without his camera, suggested we stop at Cornerstone to capture footage of the church and its history.

The moment I stepped inside, chills moved through me, as if my spirit recognized the sacred ground. I took in every detail: the weight of the doors, the richness of the wood, the craftsmanship from another era. Though well-maintained, the sanctuary carried a stillness, as if some of its former vibrancy had gone quiet.

Surrounded by glass cases displaying original letters and photographs of my great-grandfather, I was struck by the atmosphere—familiar yet distant. The scent of aged wood and polished stone evoked a deep sense of nostalgia. Though the structure had been carefully preserved, it was clear the church no longer buzzed with the same energy it once held. A maintenance worker, who let me in after learning of my connection, only reinforced the feeling that, under its current leadership, this place—once a cornerstone of the community—had become a quiet relic of the past.

As we made our way back to the car, Matt suddenly stopped. His attention had been drawn to the six-story annex beside the sanctuary, its limestone façade weathered but still dignified.

Built in 1965, the Cornerstone Baptist Church Center was established as a dual-purpose complex—housing modest residential suites and providing classrooms for adult Bible study and an innovative early childhood enrichment program. For the surrounding neighborhood, it represented hope cast in concrete and brick.

Locals soon began calling it "the crown jewel of the community." My great-grandfather had integrated an array of services, from literacy classes to a weekday hot meal program for seniors. Its corridors once rang with hymns in the morning and children's laughter in the afternoon, linking generations under one roof.

On Sunday, May 29, 1966, my great-grandfather ascended the center's front steps, joined by New York Governor Nelson A. Rockefeller and Dr. Martin Luther King Jr. Together, they cut the ceremonial ribbon and dedicated the Cornerstone Baptist Church Center "to the spiritual uplift, educational advancement, and social betterment of every resident whom its doors might welcome."

My father, Sandy F. Ray III, often told me stories of political giants, famous athletes, and celebrities who visited my great-grandfather. However, community was always at the heart of his work, inscribing the estate and our family name into the larger narrative of the civil rights era. Printed on the dedication flyer that day was a single verse: 1 Samuel 7:12. "Thus far the Lord has helped us." A quiet yet powerful reminder that every stone laid was both a memorial and a promise.

"What's this place?" Matt asked. I told him it was the residential building where seniors lived upstairs and that there was a daycare downstairs.

Then he said, "Let's go in."

I resisted. By this point, he was doing far too much exploring for my comfort, and part of me felt ashamed of how detached I had become from the legacy my family had built.

But then, that familiar whisper emerged. I took a deep breath, rang the bell, and stepped inside.

"This Is Your School."

No one was at the front desk until the Executive Director appeared from her office. I introduced myself as Jasmine Ray. Before I could even finish my sentence, she asked, "Ray? Are you related to Sandy Ray?"

"Yes," I replied. "He's my great-grandfather."

Her eyes filled with tears. "I prayed for you today," she said, her voice trembling. "We are two weeks away from closing.

I asked God to send me someone to carry this legacy. This is your school."

I stood there, stunned, trying to process what was happening. Then, the chairperson appeared, holding a stack of papers. He looked me over and said, "You're right on time. If you don't take it over, we're closing it. Technically, this is your family's school."

Still frozen in place, the weight of his words sinking in, I finally said, "I don't know anything about daycares." My voice was barely steady.

"Take the tour. We'll help you navigate it."

Later that week, the chairman called again. "If you don't want it, we'll just close it up. But this is your family's legacy. There are no other Rays around."

In that moment, my eight-year-old self flashed across my mind—seeing my great-grandfather's reflection in the glass, feeling watched over. I took a deep breath and said, "Okay. I'll take it from here."

At the time, I had been successfully running my own non-profit for five years. And although I knew very little about the world of daycare, I refused to let that deter me. There was a sense of responsibility that compelled me to step into this new role.

The appointment as the new Executive Director was met with suspicion. The deacons, trustees, and even the pastor viewed me as a trespasser—an outsider who had come out of nowhere, claiming a connection to Dr. Ray's legacy. Among the skeptics was Miss Beatrice Walls.

Her name instantly triggered a memory from when I was fourteen, visiting Cornerstone as a teenager. Back then, Miss Walls had warmly introduced herself as my great-grandfather's former secretary. She'd given me a personal tour of the church, proudly showing me a display case holding his Bible and robe, telling me these artifacts were part of my legacy—something I would one day claim.

I won't downplay how I felt when I heard she now questioned my identity. I understood the hesitation, but it still hurt. To settle the matter, I provided the board with my birth certificate, confirming my name and lineage as the daughter of Sandy F. Ray III. The revelation brought a wave of relief—and even a quiet sense of celebration—among the church members, who felt the center was finally returning to the capable hands of the Ray family.

A Trustee later held up a photo from the street-renaming ceremony. "That's you, isn't it?" And it was. I was sitting beside my mother at that event, wearing that baby blue suit—a living link to the legacy they cherished.

Yet just as I thought I'd regained Miss Walls as an ally, she passed away, and I found myself back to proving I belonged.

2018 - Rallying the Village

In the wake of her death, I began making a series of phone calls to try to halt the closing of the daycare. A local councilman I had worked with before offered to help, or so I thought. Quietly aligned with the pastor, I learned he was already showing the building to realtors. The lie revealed itself when he accidentally texted me, laying out their plan.

Unbeknownst to me, my presence had become an obstacle. Many, including the church deacons, had warned me that the pastor was mismanaging the estate finances, allowing the property to fall in disrepair and intended to sell the Cornerstone Baptist Church Education Center. Rather than helping me save the school, the councilman was feeding the pastor everything he needed to push me out.

Then I called Senator Velmanette Montgomery. Her response was immediate: "What? Jasmine Ray? Where have you guys been? Do you know your pedigree?"

I explained, "Look, Senator, I'm calling because they want to close Cornerstone Daycare."

Her reply was swift: "What? Not under my watch. We're going to ACS." Without hesitation, Senator Montgomery turned to her Chief of Staff and instructed them to call Congressman Hakeem Jeffries.

At the time, Hakeem was and still is one of the most influential Democrats in the country. When we met, he smiled with recognition. "Reverend Dr. Ray baptized me. My family and your family go way back. Whatever you need, I'm here for you."

I couldn't ignore how effortlessly these connections were aligning, how everything felt like it was coming full circle—like divine intervention.

Soon after, a letter drafted to ACS by Congressman Jeffries and signed by four powerful Black legislators opened the door. It felt as if my great-grandfather had left an indelible mark on each of them, inspiring a shared responsibility to protect not only Cornerstone but also me, as the bearer of his legacy.

Shortly after, we met with ACS Commissioner David Hansell and his deputies.

"Do you know who she is?" Senator Montgomery asked, Dashiki and all.

I sat there, confused, still wondering, *Who am I?* I didn't understand what she meant, but it felt like Auntie was in the room, scolding everyone like they were children. While I was inspired by her boldness, I couldn't fully grasp what was happening.

Some of Hansell's aides were combative, but the commissioner himself was different. Known for his deep experience and compassionate leadership, he was incredibly receptive to our pleas and deeply respectful toward the senator.

After the meeting, he bypassed everyone and walked directly to me. He leaned in and assured me he was there for whatever I needed. His graciousness and professionalism left a lasting impression. It became one of my earliest experiences witnessing the complexity of government bureaucracy balanced by true leadership at the top.

Thirty Days

The facts were ugly: non-compliance, administrative infractions, and a budget bleeding out. I stood before local leaders and pleaded, "Please give me 30 days. Let me prove this place is worth saving." Our elected officials pressed agencies and stakeholders to pause the closure. That bought us time, and I used every hour of it to bring Cornerstone into full compliance.

First stop: operations. We were severely overstaffed—twenty-one employees for a budget that couldn't breathe, especially without the student population to justify it. I met with each person one-on-one: Why are you here? How long have you been here? What are your qualifications? The truth surfaced quickly. More than half weren't a fit.

In one day, I let eleven people go, keeping the ten who had the skills and commitment to turn the school around and keep us within child-to-teacher ratios. One staffer erupted—shouting, threatening to fight, even ripping students' artwork off the walls. It only confirmed what I already knew: she didn't belong there. I let the tantrum burn out, then she left. And then we got back to work.

Next came the funding. Three consultants were draining the budget without delivering value; I cut them. I also released the Executive Director who brought me in; her salary load was unsustainable. It hurt, but it was the only path to survival, and she graciously understood that.

Thirty days later, we weren't guessing anymore. We were compliant, correctly staffed, and finally operating like a school with a future.

Building Forward

One of the true perks Cornerstone Daycare Center enjoyed was the privilege of having a full-scale industrial kitchen on site—a rarity among schools in our community. Even more special was the fact that the meals were prepared each day by a local elder, whose presence in the kitchen connected our children not only to nourishment but to tradition. While many other schools relied on pre-packaged meals delivered by large distributors, our children had the advantage of food that was fresh, cooked, and rooted in the hands of someone who cared about their well-being.

Recognizing this unique opportunity, I knew it was time to take a bold step. I made the swift decision to completely overhaul our menu. Processed foods were eliminated. White rice was replaced with brown rice. French fries to sweet potatoes. I banned all canned or pre-packaged fruit and mandated that we cut fresh fruit, daily. I even implemented a no-sugar policy for birthday parties and holidays. The snacks that had once been loaded with sugar and empty calories were substituted with wholesome alternatives.

While these were easy fixes, one of the most serious failures was that the center had no licensed teacher which is a legal requirement in New York. This wasn't babysitting; it was a learning center. I immediately hired a retired DOE-licensed teacher and former school Principal to own the curriculum and coach the staff. I even took a smaller salary than hers because she was the anchor the school needed. She led instruction; I rebuilt operations.

By the end of year two, Cornerstone was thriving. I was able to negotiate a healthy budget at the top of the fiscal year and we invested every dollar where it mattered: new furniture, a website, updated computers, smart boards, and a tablets for every classroom. We weren't just preserving tradition; we were building the future.

But while I was focused on rebuilding Cornerstone, a personal turmoil was quietly brewing—one that would soon demand its own kind of rebuilding.

***

2019

I was renovating a house I had just purchased in Pennsylvania, which meant commuting back and forth between PA and NY. Meanwhile, my fiancé, unwilling to hold a steady job, wasn't contributing much. I became the pillar holding everything together, the backbone of it all, while managing Cornerstone. At the same time, I volunteered for Mayor Bill de Blasio's administration in the early childhood sector. Despite the added responsibility, I was deeply proud of the work I was doing.

My decision to volunteer was inspired by the introduction of Universal Pre-Kindergarten (UPK) in 2014—a bold initiative by de Blasio's administration aimed at providing free, high-quality early education for all four-year-olds in New York City. For parents like me, it was life-changing. The program was ambitious and politically challenging, but I saw it as a beacon of hope for families in need.

At the time, I was a single mother living on Staten Island's North Shore, juggling the financial strain of paying $975 a month in tuition because I wanted the best early education for my son, even if it meant making sacrifices.

I'll never forget the morning I dropped him off at Kiddie Academy on the South Shore. As I walked in, I prepared myself for the usual transaction. But as I went to pay, the administrator smiled and waved me over.

"You don't have to pay anymore," she said, eyes bright with excitement. "School is free now."

My breath caught in my throat, and tears welled up in my eyes. It wasn't just about the money. It was about what this moment meant for my son's future, for our stability, and for the thousands of families across the city who could now breathe a little easier.

This was one of the first times an election felt personal. The de Blasio administration's decisions, especially UPK, were shaping lives like mine—turning uncertainty into real opportunity. It was a clear reminder that political choices don't stay on campaign stages; they land in kitchens and classrooms and paychecks, touching everyday families.

2020

The sudden shift to remote learning during the pandemic exposed deep disparities in access and forced many centers, including mine, to temporarily close. We had to navigate these complexities from a distance, ensuring that Universal Pre-K continued to serve New York City's children—even as we were also classified as essential workers.

We engaged in weekly conversations with then–Deputy Chancellor Josh Wallack, and over time, those interactions evolved into friendships grounded in transparency. I admired the de Blasio administration's commitment to early childhood education, especially as they launched initiatives many believed were impossible.

But while Cornerstone was healing, my home was fraying. The work gave me purpose, but it also consumed me. In the quiet moments, when the Zoom calls ended and the classrooms went dark, I was left alone to face the realities of my personal life.

***

People are undeniably shaped by their experiences. Although Matt and I grew up just minutes apart on the

North Shore of Staten Island, our upbringings were worlds apart. He was raised in NYCHA housing, where survival and resourcefulness were the focus, while I grew up in a single-family home. We met at age 11 and shared our first date at 13, weaving in and out of each other's lives throughout our youth. It wasn't until our 30s that we decided to truly commit to a relationship.

Despite our closeness, the differences in our backgrounds created a widening gap. Where I saw life as something to build upon, he often saw it as something to survive. His habit of unwinding with drinks at every celebration felt foreign to me. My family didn't drink or smoke—a stark contrast that underscored how differently our environments had shaped us.

Even the little things we gravitated toward in our downtime revealed the divide. His family could sit in a room and talk for hours about "back in the day." He always made jokes referencing *Martin*, the cult-classic show that shaped a generation, while I had never sat through a single episode. I, on the other hand, grew up watching *I Love Lucy* and my family spent hours playing Monopoly. Our worlds, though both valid, had left us with fundamentally different outlooks on life, making it hard to bridge the gap.

That disconnect, rooted in something deeper than habits, was at the heart of why our relationship couldn't survive.

Still, I was excited and eager to start a new chapter as a family. During the pandemic in 2020, we temporarily relocated to my property in Pennsylvania, trying to escape the harsh reality of NYC's COVID-19 restrictions. I was pregnant at the time, and earlier that year, he had proposed to me on a beach in Puerto Rico.

2021

In April 2021, we welcomed our daughter. Life was overwhelming, but I convinced myself this new beginning would fix everything—or so I thought. I was excited, imagining the life we were building, until a text message shattered the moment. While we were food shopping, I glanced at my phone, and a photo of my fiancé's penis filled the screen. Shock hit first, then a wave of shame. I turned the phone and quietly showed him. For me, betrayal has a sound. It is silent.

I pride myself on staying calm and measured, never seeking vengeance, but instead channeling my energy into becoming a better version of myself. And that's exactly what I did. It wouldn't have made sense to legally commit to a new chapter with someone who had already shown disloyalty and proved himself untrustworthy. Although we continued living under the same roof, the burden of everything fell squarely on my shoulders.

Still, I planned on staying and working through it, hoping things would change. I was managing the household and the business, and the constant pressure of our circumstances. I was breastfeeding, postpartum, overweight and overwhelmed. Despite my best efforts, it all came to a breaking point. One day, during a heated debate, Matt dropped a bomb that shattered everything. His words hit me like a wrecking ball: he told me he was never in love with me.

I immediately asked, "So why did you propose?"

His response was cold and indifferent: "It seemed like the right thing to do."

The emotional devastation came crashing down like a freight train, and my body followed suit. A crushing heaviness settled in my chest, as if the truth had physically broken me. In the days that followed, my body couldn't keep up. The stress and heartbreak were so severe that my breastmilk stopped flowing. Not a single drop. It felt like everything I had been giving, everything I had been holding onto, had been completely emptied. It wasn't just pain; it was collapse. Total exhaustion that went far beyond the emotional.

This collapse mirrored a moment during my pregnancy with Poem when I had felt equally powerless. I had chosen a natural approach to childbirth, believing in the body's inherent strength and opting for a midwife over medication, sonograms, and needles. It was a deeply personal decision, rooted in my belief that our bodies can heal and grow without external interference. But the journey wasn't without its challenges.

Everything had been progressing smoothly until labor began. Despite spending a long time in the birthing pool, Poem just wouldn't descend. The midwife, after assessing the situation, said, "She should've come out by now. You need to go to the hospital." I was devastated. Everything I had planned, all the preparation with the midwife and the costs involved, felt like it was all going down the drain. In that moment, I knew I had no choice but to go.

At the hospital, my condition rapidly deteriorated. I was fainting, losing consciousness, and waking up in a fog. The medical team informed me that Poem was losing oxygen. A C-section was no longer a question; it was a necessity.

The surgery was grueling. I was highly sensitive to anesthesia, and my body rejected it, causing me to vomit uncontrollably. I've always avoided medication, so this reaction was overwhelming and left me feeling powerless. As the procedure continued, I overheard the doctor instructing a group of students who were shadowing him. At that moment, I felt like a mere subject in an experiment—someone being used to train others at the expense of my own dignity and well-being. The operating room was chaotic, with staff rushing around, while I couldn't see what was happening to me.

Yet Poem, my strong, beautiful baby, was resilient. Born at 8 pounds, 8 oz and 21 inches, she was a stallion of a baby—remarkably healthy despite everything. She spat out her own mucus, took her first breaths, and immediately began showcasing her motor skills and stepping reflex seconds after emerging. The nurses were enamored by her. She was a fighter, and in that moment, so was I.

While Poem was healthy and strong, the aftermath of the surgery was far from over. During delivery, my incision extended into a 4-centimeter tear in the lower uterine segment, a complication that was not explained to me at the hospital, but by my midwife weeks later after she reviewed the OR report. The tear led to significant bleeding — I lost a full liter of blood before it was controlled.

My hospital stay stretched on much longer than expected. I was clouded by uncertainty about what had actually happened to my body, yet aware that in that moment, something felt wrong. While grateful for a healthy baby, the betrayal I felt toward the doctors and the system were indescribable.

In the United States, Black women are three to four times more likely to die from pregnancy-related causes than White women. In 2021, the maternal mortality rate for non-Hispanic Black women was 69.9 deaths per 100,000 live births, compared to 26.6 for non-Hispanic White women. These disparities stem from a combination of implicit racial bias in healthcare, lack of access to quality care, and underlying chronic health conditions prevalent in Black communities.

My experience was a stark reminder of these systemic issues. While I was fortunate to survive, many Black women do not. The healthcare system's failure to properly support and protect Black mothers is not just a statistic; it is a crisis — one that demands urgent attention and meaningful change.

What I experienced in childbirth, though a completely different kind of pain, felt eerily similar to the devastation I felt when Matt told me he didn't love me. Both were jarring revelations that shattered my sense of self, leaving me helpless and exposed. The rawness of it all, feeling broken in ways I never expected, was something I hadn't prepared for.

As the weight of Matt's betrayal settled, I realized the timing couldn't have been more perfect. Too perfect, almost. Just as I was closing one chapter, ending one relationship, destiny—disguised as heartbreak—came rushing in. It was a force that would propel me forward, onto a new path. And it arrived in the form of a message.

For five long years after my breakup with Eric, there was silence between us. We had no line of communication. On holidays, I'd occasionally hear from him, but my responses were either nonexistent or, at best, one-word replies. I had intentionally distanced myself, closing off the world he was building while I tried to rebuild mine. His life felt like a distant memory.

Then, just a few days after Matt broke my heart, my phone lit up. It was him—the one I had silently grieved, the one my heart still carried in its deepest corners. His message stopped me cold:

"I just won the primary. I'm going to be Mayor of New York City, and I don't want to do this without you."

And then he called.

CHAPTER 7 - FLAWED HERO

In a world so quick to judge, I've come to see cancel culture for what it often is: a knee-jerk reaction rooted in anger, fear, and ego. It masquerades as righteousness but rarely leaves room for growth, redemption, or the complexity of being human.

This understanding was tested in real time as I watched Eric navigate an increasingly unforgiving political landscape. The contradictions began early, when he publicly claimed to be a vegan—only to be photographed eating fish. To some, it was a harmless slip. To others, it was proof of a larger fraud. That single moment planted a seed of doubt, giving critics license to question his every move, every word, and even his integrity.

And yet, isn't that the burden of leadership? To have your humanity scrutinized until even your smallest flaws are weaponized?

From federal charges that were eventually dismissed to the bold move of announcing his re-election campaign as an independent candidate, Eric has often stood at the center of controversy. His handling of the migrant crisis began with a welcoming tone, then became more guarded as the strain on the city's resources grew undeniable. That shift earned him the label of a walking contradiction. His direct way of speaking and frequent clashes with the press only sharpened public opinion against him.

If you ask people what fuels their dislike of Eric, the answers come quickly.

"He's arrogant."

"He lies."

"He's rude."

"He can't even speak properly."

They'll mock the way he talks, laugh at his slip-ups, and treat every misstep as proof he's unfit. What rarely gets mentioned, if at all, is his lifelong battle with dyslexia.

Dyslexia doesn't disappear with age. It doesn't graduate with you or dissolve once you're in a position of power. It shows up in moments of public speaking, in the stress of interviews, and in the everyday act of finding the right words in real time. And yet, most people never consider that the very things they ridicule may stem from something deeper—something they can't see.

Eric isn't the first NYC leader to carry a visible or invisible difference, and he won't be the last. David Paterson served as governor while legally blind, never asking for pity, only respect. New York City Public Advocate Jumaane Williams, who I consider a friend, lives with Tourette's and has been unapologetically vocal about what that means in leadership. And then there's Eric, showing up day after day, carrying the reality of dyslexia—a condition that doesn't bow to titles or power.

These men show us something important: that real leadership doesn't come from flawlessness. It comes from facing the world exactly as you are and choosing to lead anyway.

Studies show that many adults with dyslexia, like Eric, carry low self-esteem, diminished self-efficacy, and higher anxiety—especially when they lack empathy for themselves. Research by Niolaki et al. (2025) found that a crucial factor is "over-identification," which refers to obsessing over personal failures and directly heightens anxiety.

Think of that "chip on the shoulder," the forceful swagger, the hurried speech. These aren't just political theatrics; they are coping mechanisms. Eric likely learned early to stand tall, speak loudly, and build a shield around himself to silence the internal critic that labeled him "dumb."

Traits like confidence used as armor, a guarded posture, and sometimes a brash delivery can easily be misread as arrogance. But the science says otherwise. They are survival tools—shaped by a brain trained to over-identify with its mistakes and a heart that isn't allowed to fall apart, even when it's trembling inside.

Eric's journey taught me something I didn't fully understand until I saw it up close: leadership was never about perfection. It's about resilience, accountability, and the quiet, stubborn ability to grow in real time, even when the world isn't patient enough to wait for you to unfold.

This idea isn't new. History is full of leaders who carried both greatness and imperfection.

John F. Kennedy is still revered for his vision during the Civil Rights Movement and the Space Race, though his personal life was entangled in controversy. Bill Clinton presided over a period of economic growth, yet his presidency bears the shadow of scandal.

Even closer to home, New York has had its share of leaders whose legacies are complicated by personal scandal. Eliot Spitzer rose to power as the "Sheriff of Wall Street," celebrated for taking on corruption with fearless intensity. Yet his governorship ended in disgrace when a prostitution scandal forced him to resign. Years later, Andrew Cuomo would follow a similar path—once praised for his steady hand during the pandemic, he ultimately stepped down after allegations of sexual misconduct. Both men left behind a mix of progress and disappointment, reminders that greatness and frailty often walk hand in hand.

These examples reveal an essential truth: leadership is not defined by the absence of flaws, but by the resilience to move through them, the accountability to face them, and the courage to keep growing while the world is watching.

If we want a more compassionate society, we must begin by modeling that compassion ourselves—because grace extended outward has a way of returning inward. And perhaps that's what makes a flawed hero still worthy of the title. It isn't perfection that defines them, but persistence in the pursuit of something greater than themselves.

Long before I came to understand what a flawed hero looked like in politics, I had already lived with one. My earliest lessons in strength, imperfection, and love came from the man I first called a hero: my father.

***

I was raised by a proud Black man. He stood a solid 5′10″, with a thick afro, a broad nose, and a presence that was unmistakably and unapologetically Black. He party grew up in a Jewish community in Brooklyn, and their influence rubbed off on him in subtle ways. His peers sometimes teased him, saying he "didn't talk Black." My Dad excelled at tennis, listened to jazz and gravitated toward artists like Stealy Dan. But my father was Black-Black—the kind of Black that wore his heritage like armor, with a soul rooted in something deep and unshakable. He had once been raised like a prince, and by the time I came along, he had grown into a king.

His grandfather, Reverend Dr. Sandy Ray, whom I reference often in this book, was more than a local legend. His influence stretched far beyond Brooklyn, shaping lives across cities, congregations, and generations. Because of that lineage, my father moved through life with a quiet, effortless sense of royalty.

Yet for all the stature he came from, success is still an individual journey. Legacy can open doors, but it doesn't walk the path for you. My father's life wasn't easy. And maybe that's what gave him such wisdom and humility to pass down. He had seen enough highs and lows to know what truly mattered, and he carried those lessons like treasures he couldn't wait to share.

In the early years of my childhood, we went on countless road trips—sometimes across states, sometimes just long drives that seemed to stretch forever. Those moments became sacred. That's when he slowed down enough to really pour into us. The car would fill with his voice, steady and sure, as he spoke about life, the world, and everything he had come to understand along the way.

"Be humble," he'd say. "Nobody's better than you, but you're no better than anyone else." He said it so often it became a rhythm in my head—something I'd carry for the rest of my life. And there was always more: "You have to know a little about everything. Be well-rounded in culture, politics, art, science, and whatever you do."

That was my father. He always pushed us to be both grounded and expansive, never letting us forget who we were or what we could become.

As serious as he could be when it came time to pour guidance and care into his children, he was also the perfect balance of a man. He could shift from teacher to playmate in an instant. My dad was endlessly playful. When appropriate, everything with him became a game. Even in the middle of a deep conversation, he'd pivot and test me: "Name this artist," he'd say with a grin, or toss out little challenges to keep me sharp.

He was an enigma in every sense: a philosopher and a jokester, humble yet commanding, hard to define but impossible to forget in any room he entered.

On weekends, while my mother went out with her friends, my dad became the center of our world. He'd gather us and the kids of my mom's friends, creating magic out of the ordinary. He took us to the video store, picked out scary movies like *Freddy Krueger*, and pushed all the sofas together to make a giant bed we could pile onto. Then he'd fire up the kitchen and host a full-blown fish fry, frying endless plates of shrimp, fish, and French fries until the whole house smelled like love.

He built tents in the living room, handed out plates of food, and let us scream and laugh our way through the night as the movies played. He watched us with a face full of joy and character, completely in his element. Everyone wanted to sleep over our house because of him. He wasn't just a father to me and my brother; he was a force in the lives of others, too. In those moments, he felt like a flawless hero.

But the truth is, no hero is without flaw.

As much of a hero as he was in our eyes, my dad was also a deeply flawed man. He struggled to hold down steady jobs but not due to a lack of drive. My father was never lazy, not by a mile. He had battled his demons early in life, a struggle that began when he got caught up in the 1980s crack epidemic. By the time he was raising me, he'd long been clean, but there were still remnants of that past life.

He didn't have a strong skill set to lean on, and the only work available to him was jobs, not lasting careers.

But where he fell short as a provider, he more than made up for it in presence. While my mother worked, my dad was home with us—hands-on in a way that left an indelible mark on who we became. He made it his mission to shape us into the best humans and athletes we could be. Day after day, he'd toss a softball to me with quiet determination, repeating the drill until it became second nature. He was fully intent on making me the greatest player I could be. And I can proudly say he succeeded in that regard.

That was the kind of father he was: present, attentive, and relentless in his love, even if he wasn't always the provider he wanted to be. And though a man may be flawed, the moments when he shows up as a hero should echo louder than any mistake he's made.

I recall one afternoon, standing in the outfield at my softball game. I played for Our Lady of Perpetual Help (OLPH), in Sunset Park. This particular day I had no family in the stands, unlike most of the other kids, because both of my parents had to work. It didn't feel good knowing I was there alone, but I pushed the feeling down and told myself: *You've got to swing big anyway.*

It was a sunny day—the kind where the heat wraps around you like a heavy blanket. Sweat beaded along my brow, rolling down the side of my face as the sun pressed hard against the back of my neck.

I took a deep breath and stepped out in front of the catcher. The sound of the traffic behind us faded to a low, distant hum. Having pretty good accuracy, during this moment, I have a habit of pointing at my target with my bat, letting the opposing team know in advance where I intended to hit the ball. It was arrogant. I know. But in this moment I know nothing but belief — that even arrogance has its place when it comes wrapped in courage and timing.

I adjusted my cap the way Dad taught me, tightened my grip on the bat, and planted my feet. And though I felt the absence of familiar faces, I steadied myself anyway.

I bent my knees, locked in my stance, stared down the pitcher like I had something to prove, and got ready to crush the ball.

And then, just as the pitcher wound up, I heard it.

"Let's go, Jas!"

My heart leapt.

I turned my head and there he was—my dad—standing just beyond the field in his brown UPS uniform. He had left his route, parked his truck along the edge of the field, and showed up at the exact moment it mattered most.

A smile stretched across my face so wide it felt like the whole field could see it. Suddenly, I wasn't just the kid with no family in the stands. I was unstoppable. Nothing felt better than seeing my Dad there, making me feel like the most important player on earth.

That day reminded me of a truth I carry even now: even the most imperfect men can still have heroic timing.

When I was twelve years old, my parents divorced, and my dad packed up his life and moved to North Carolina.

A few months later, he came back to New York with a look in his eyes I'll never forget.

"Let's go. You're coming with me," he said.

I cried hard, stubborn tears. Leaving New York felt like leaving my whole world behind. But he didn't flinch. "It's not up for debate. You're coming with me."

And that was that.

Moving from Staten Island, New York City, to Drexel, North Carolina, was like stepping into an entirely different world. The drive alone felt like a slow unraveling of everything I had ever known. As the miles passed, towering buildings gave way to open land. The streets widened, and the cars shifted from yellow cabs and constant traffic to pickup trucks and quiet roads. Even the air felt different. It was softer, warmer, and less rushed. It didn't just smell cleaner; it felt cleaner.

Time seemed to slow down, and for the first time, I could actually hear myself think. I felt the stillness of a place that wasn't trying to prove anything. A place that didn't demand your hustle, just your presence.

In the beginning, my nights in our new home were restless. Anyone born and raised in New York City knows that the chaos—the sirens, the shouting, the constant energy of life—is oddly comforting. It's the noise that rocks us to sleep. So when all of that disappeared and was replaced by stillness, it felt unsettling. The quiet wasn't peaceful at first; it was loud in its own way. But over time, I adapted. I learned to breathe in the silence, and eventually, I grew within it. That quiet taught me something city noise never could: how to sit with myself, how to find comfort in solitude, and how to hear the world when it isn't begging you to keep moving.

When we moved down South, we didn't have much. There were nights when all we had for dinner was rice, cooked in the microwave with water. Though I was young and didn't fully grasp the depth of my father's struggle, I could feel the edges of it in small moments like that. I still remember the fear that crept over me when the repo man came knocking for his car. My Dad would park it blocks away so they couldn't find it, but that only made them come back—pounding on the door, harassing him constantly.

He struggled, yes—but ironically, life with my father never felt like a struggle. Somehow, he gave us a childhood that felt rich in all the ways that count.

When I was about fifteen, my brother and I accidentally started a small fire in the woods that got out of control. We left before realizing the extent of what we had caused. Later, the fire department showed up at our door, suspecting kids had been involved.

When they left, we sat in silence, bracing ourselves for Dad's wrath. But the explosion never came. He didn't yell, didn't lecture, didn't raise a hand.

Instead, he broke down crying and walked out the door.

There's nothing more heartbreaking than seeing a grown man cry, especially your father. It stopped us in our tracks and cut through all the noise of our teenage defiance. From that day forward, my brother and I straightened up. Everything from our grades to our sibling rivalry shifted. There was no more fighting, no more ruckus, no more chaos. We just wanted to be our best for the man who was always his best for us.

Looking back now, I wonder if there was more behind those tears than just frustration over two reckless kids. Maybe it was something deeper—old pain and heavy sorrows that had finally spilled over. Whatever the source, his tears alone were enough to make us wake up and get it together.

It was during the most critical years of my life that my father raised me. I went back and forth between New York and North Carolina so many times it felt like my life was split in two. At 12, I was there. At 14, I was back. At 16, I left again. And by 18, I graduated from East Burke High School in Icard, NC.

Somewhere in the middle of all that, I got my first job working as a cook and caterer at Myra's in Valdese, the town next to Drexel. Myra's is known for its smash burgers and ice cream. It was small-town work with big lessons, and it rooted me in ways I didn't yet understand.

Ultimately, being caught between two cities made it hard to hold on to friendships. I was always starting over—never staying in one place long enough to build lasting bonds or finish a chapter with the people I started it with. It left an imprint on me and shaped the way I navigate relationships even now.

Back then, I had to train myself not to cling to people or have high hopes for new connections. One school year, I'd grow close to someone, and by the next, I'd be pulled away when it was time to return to New York. Over time, I developed an almost automatic ability to detach—an unconscious way of protecting myself from the pain of letting go.

It wasn't about being cold. It was about surviving.

If you had to choose between heartbreak and self-preservation, what would you choose?

***

In time, my father faced one of the hardest seasons of his life. He had fallen on tough times and, for a while, didn't have much to his name. It was painful to witness someone I loved so deeply reach such a low point, especially someone who had poured so much of himself into our childhood. But life has a way of coming full circle.

Shortly after high school, I was signed by Tommy Mottola to Casablana/Universal Records. That record deal, along with a lucrative "back to school" JC Penny commercial began earning a generous income through my music royalties. Being in a position to support my Dad felt like more than a financial victory; it was an emotional one. I was able to send him lump sums when he needed them most, and it filled my heart with gratitude to give back to the man who, despite his struggles, had always shown up for me in the ways that mattered.

By the time he turned forty, he was fed up. He had grown tired of the struggle and weary from the endless cycle of odd jobs. Earlier in life, he had served three years in the military, but that chapter felt long behind him. One day, he hit his breaking point and said, "I can't live like this anymore."

So he started over—slowly, quietly, and with a determination that still makes me beam with pride to this day. He went back to school, earned his Bachelor of Arts in Social Sciences, and later went on to earn his Master's in Special Education. He became a teacher for children with special needs, spending his days doing the kind of work that requires patience, compassion, and a steady heart. For twenty years, he poured himself into the public school system, showing up every single day for kids who needed someone to believe in them.

When he retired, he did so on his own terms. He paid off his car, bought a house, and carved out a life of peace for himself. These days, he spends his mornings playing pickleball and his afternoons enjoying the slower pace of life in Sanford, North Carolina.

My father found his way.

A flawed hero—not because he was perfect, but because he kept trying, even when life gave him every reason to give up.

And maybe that's what heroism really is. Not the absence of mistakes, but the persistence to grow beyond them.

My father showed me that truth first. Eric reminded me of it in real time.

Two Black men from New York City. Both shaped by hardship, both deeply imperfect, both choosing to rise anyway. One shaped my childhood; the other challenged my perspective on power, leadership, and grace. Neither asked to be idolized, only to be seen fully—flaws and all.

So when I look at Eric, I no longer search for perfection. I search for persistence, growth, and the courage it takes to lead while still learning. Just like my father, he is a flawed hero. And maybe that's the only kind that truly exists.

CHAPTER 8 - PUBLIC PERCEPTION

In this age where the media shapes every narrative, the truth often gets lost in a haze of smoke and mirrors. What the public sees—and what they're led to believe—is rarely the full picture. Headlines pull attention toward drama and controversy while burying the real issues out of sight.

Public perception isn't built on facts but on images designed for mass consumption. The media holds the mic. It stirs emotion, crowns heroes, builds villains, and drives conversations that can make or break a reputation. A single article can snowball into a storyline so widespread it feels impossible to escape.

Reporters, with all their boldness, ask questions with an agenda, then clip the answers, releasing only fragments that fit the narrative they've already decided to tell. The raw moments are magnified, and clarity is buried. Stories are framed to provoke outrage, admiration, or indifference, and reality gets lost in translation.

This is the machine I've witnessed up close.

And yet, though this may come as a surprise, I can't bring myself to hate it. Everyone has a role in society, and the media's is critical. Without it, corruption would go unchecked, and the ruling class would move in silence with no accountability. Freedom of the press, though often unfair, is essential. Reporters and editors are often the first line of defense against injustice, shining a light on what others would prefer to keep hidden. Without them, who would uncover the facts buried beneath the lies?

But like any tool, the media's power depends on how it's wielded. In the wrong hands, it misleads and manipulates; in the right hands, it educates, empowers, and exposes what's real. I've seen both sides of that coin, and I've felt the weight when the scale tips the wrong direction.

The Power of the Narrative

On the national stage, relentless coverage of President Donald Trump shaped public opinion and fueled polarization. In New York City, the press corps applied the same playbook to Eric. From his first days in office, they didn't just report on his actions; they scrutinized him, as if waiting for the moment he would slip. It wasn't simply about politics; it was about turning him into a character for public consumption, where every move could be dissected and spun into something more than it was.

When the 57-page indictment dropped, full of accusations about airline upgrades and straw donations, the charges themselves were relatively minor. But the press didn't present them that way. Instead of contextualizing, they cherry-picked and inflated details, stripping away nuance. What could have been dismissed as petty became a spectacle. Headlines used words like *scandal* and *corruption*, sending a message of guilt rather than due process.

The reality is, most people don't read indictments. They skim headlines, absorb summaries, and form impressions in seconds. In an age of information overload, it's a shortcut. But those shortcuts stick. The emotional reaction to a headline often outlasts the facts.

That's the danger of legacy media. They've mastered the use of soundbites and strategic framing—not balanced storytelling. It's less about uncovering accuracy and more about manufacturing outrage. I watched this happen in real time with Eric. Every action was recast as part of a pre-determined storyline. Accusations were amplified; defenses ignored. The portrait wasn't one of integrity or context; it was of someone who, at best, was compromised and, at worst, a criminal.

This isn't journalism. It's machinery. A system that stretches fragments of actuality into spectacle, distorting them until they're unrecognizable, while ensuring the public's attention lands exactly where they want it.

***

It wasn't the first time this played out, but it was one of the clearest.

On February 14, 2025, what was billed as a long-awaited and high-stakes meeting between Eric and former Border Czar Tom Homan finally took place live on *Fox & Friends*. Given their rocky history, the moment was more than symbolic; it marked unexpected progress. Homan had publicly criticized Eric multiple times, accusing him of failing to act on public safety threats and other urgent issues. However, in this interview, the two men sat down not as adversaries but as leaders determined to find common ground for the sake of New York City.

"I've called the mayor out many times for not stepping up on public safety," Homan admitted during the segment. "But when I sat down with him, I saw the cop in him, and he really does want to do the right thing. He is a cop, he's a lifelong cop, and he's serious about making this city safer."

Despite their political differences and past tensions, Homan made it clear that he saw something real in Eric that day—a deep commitment to public service and a shared desire to improve the city. Together, they laid out collaborative plans to address crime, safety, and civic order. This wasn't performative politics. It was two sides coming together: Eric, a Democrat, and Homan, a Republican and former Trump official, setting aside past disagreements to have a real, productive conversation about solutions.

At the very end of the segment, as they wrapped up on a note of mutual respect, Homan made a lighthearted joke:

"If he doesn't come through, I'll be back in NYC, and we won't be sitting on his couch. I'll be in his office, up his butt, saying, 'Where the hell is the agreement we came to?'"

And just like that, a new narrative was born.

Homan's comment was a moment of levity. It was simply his rough-around-the-edges way of saying, "I'm holding you accountable, man." However, legacy media didn't care about the progress, the partnership, or the substance of the conversation. By the next morning, the headlines had nothing to do with unity. They zeroed in on that one line—and that alone.

It went viral. And just like that, Eric was branded as "Trump's boy." The same outlets that ignored the heart of the dialogue amplified the soundbite and buried the bigger story under mockery and misinformation.

That's how quickly perception can shift. What began as a joke meant to signal accountability became a clipped moment that transformed the entire narrative, turning partnership into propaganda.

The Human Cost

While it isn't entirely fair to place the blame solely on the press, it's crucial to recognize the immense power the media wields and how continuous negative coverage can shape public perception in ways that ripple far beyond the leader in question. The consequences aren't confined to one person or one office. When the press consistently paints a negative picture, it doesn't just hurt Eric; it harms all of us.

Think about it this way: just as a sports team rallies behind its captain for the greater good, a city and a nation must come together in support of their leaders. They're the ones steering the ship through uncharted waters, and if we're too quick to tear them down, we risk destabilizing the very foundation they're trying to strengthen. Undermining a leader doesn't just create a power vacuum; it cultivates an environment of mistrust and division.

When the media repeatedly tears down a figurehead, it doesn't just bruise an ego; it reshapes the culture. Leadership stops looking like collaboration or principled debate and starts to feel like a blood sport. Trust between leaders and the communities they serve erodes. And with that erosion, the foundation of progress begins to crack.

This isn't a local problem; it's a national reflex. A media ecosystem that rewards controversy, sensationalism, and spectacle doesn't merely skew perception; it hardens it. The result is a public trained to see opponents as enemies, to mistake volume for truth, and to accept outrage as evidence.

What lesson does that teach the next generation of leaders, who watch reputations destroyed before facts are known? What does it do to our faith in institutions, in one another, in the possibility of a common good? Division isn't just noisy; it's dangerous. And when rhetoric dehumanizes, violence is no longer unthinkable. It becomes imaginable.

At some point, we have to ask: Who benefits when we tear our leaders down? What are we really achieving when we let the media frame every story as a battle for public opinion instead of a chance for honest dialogue and understanding?

The Title IX Firestorm

I experienced firsthand how swiftly the media can reshape a story in February 2025, when I took to Instagram to share my support for Title IX and President Trump's executive order. Officially titled "Keeping Men Out of Women's Sports," the order directed federal agencies to interpret Title IX as prohibiting transgender girls and women from competing in girls' and women's sports. It also threatened to withhold federal funding from schools and athletic programs that failed to comply.

My intention was simple: to support women's sports and ensure fairness in competition. As the Director of Sports Wellness and Recreation for the City of New York, I saw it as my duty to make sure all athletes, regardless of gender, could compete safely and fairly. And as a woman, that responsibility carried even greater weight.

But there was another layer. After repeated warnings from Eric about how corrupt and "evil" the press corps could be, I wanted to see for myself just how deep the rabbit hole went. So I poked them. And when I did, the response came swiftly—fueled by more distortion and disinformation than I could have ever anticipated.

The backlash was immediate. Articles began circulating, accusing me of being transphobic. A New York City Councilmember even called for my resignation. Outlets like *Gothamist* painted my stance as hateful, and the media quickly piled on, casting me as a villain in a cultural war that had little to do with my actual intentions. For the most part, I got my answer, and I can't say Eric was wrong in warning me.

Let me be clear: Title IX is a landmark law designed to protect the rights of women in education and athletics. It was created to ensure women have access to the same opportunities as men—one of the bedrocks of gender equity in this country. Yet all of that got lost in the noise. People didn't hear the full context of what I was trying to say; they only heard the labels.

And let me be equally clear: I have no phobia toward anyone or anything. I was raised to be open-minded and free of hate. I don't need to agree with someone's perspective to respect them, extend grace, or recognize their humanity.

I acknowledge that part of the confusion was on me. In my original Instagram story, I wrote, "For those asking about my position, as Director of NYC Sports & Recreation, I stand with the recent executive order..." That language blurred the line between personal belief and professional duty. I quickly and publicly clarified the misstep in a statement to Gothamist. I understood it was irresponsible, as a leader, to defy city policy, and for that, I was reprimanded. Still, the response and false accusations felt excessively harsh, aggressive, and completely uncalled for.

For me, it was a wake-up call and preparation for the potential response to this book, especially this chapter.

The Cost of Headlines

What's rarely considered is the human cost of media scrutiny. Relentless coverage of public figures can chip away at a person's spirit, drain their energy, and leave them questioning their worth.

I'm a mother of two, an advocate, a public servant, the daughter of a teacher, the niece of a police officer, and the great-granddaughter of one of this nation's greatest orators. But in that moment, none of it mattered. I became political fodder, a tool to bait the public into furthering the narrative that the administration was corrupt. It was a calculated move to discredit not just my work, but my character.

In February 2025, Eric was walking out of Bellevue Hospital and stopped briefly to take pictures with his constituents, when a group of reporters closed in. For two weeks straight, he'd canceled his regular Q&A sessions at

City Hall. At the time, the political pressure on him was immense, and he hadn't yet addressed the DOJ dropping his charges or the resignations of our four Deputy Mayors—a development that hurt him deeply. Still, instead of facing the press, he chose to visit a wounded police officer—another quiet nod to his care for real people, even as headlines raged around him.

And, true to form, that's what drew the most attention. Not the dropped charges. Not the internal chaos he was managing. The focus became the visit itself—the optics of a photo op—and the fact that he wasn't standing at a podium feeding them soundbites.

Outside the hospital, amid the press frenzy, reporter Katy Honan asked, "Why don't you take questions from the press?"

Eric's response was sharp and unfiltered: "Because you're liars." The clip exploded online.

Later that week, in an NY1 interview, Honan claimed the real issue was his refusal to give the press an opportunity to ask questions. But is he wrong? If the truth is constantly twisted, distorted, and turned into something unrecognizable—what's the crime in not wanting to be interviewed?

***

While I respect the media and understand its role, Eric doesn't share that sentiment. From his perspective, the press can't be trusted. Their mission, as he sees it, is to tear people down, especially those who don't fit the mold or play by their rules. And after witnessing how he's been treated firsthand, and living through my own little "social experiment" with Title IX, I can't say I blame him.

Eric's Communications Director often said, "One of Eric's biggest missteps was never fully learning how to tell his own story." That lack of storytelling often left him at a disadvantage. His achievements weren't amplified in the press, and without a clear narrative from him, the media was free to define it instead.

The consequence is clear: the media controls the narrative, and he doesn't. This is where public perception begins to cut both ways. There are invaluable lessons in knowing how and when not to fight the press. Eric's constant battles only gave oxygen to the negative. But what might have happened if he had taken a step back, reintroduced himself, and reclaimed the story on his own terms?

Would the media have still found a way to twist his message and misrepresent his actions? Probably. But at least he would've owned more of the narrative along the way.

The Complexity of ELA

Eric's media portrayal was cemented before he even took office—beginning during his campaign, when critics and commentators rushed to define him without ever truly hearing him. Even then, I could see the story being shaped before he had the chance to speak for himself.

A friend of mine was present the night he won the primary, just before he was scheduled to appear on a popular NYC-based podcast. Before Eric even arrived, she overheard the interview team huddled together, strategizing how they would corner him, attack his stop-and-frisk policy, and "get him with the facts."

However, within minutes of the interview, every dart—every pointed question—was dismantled as Eric responded with clarity, breaking down his mission and policies. By the end, the tone had completely shifted. The interview closed with newfound supporters—people whose hearts were full of hope at the thought of a great man of color leading the city, despite having doubted him just an hour earlier.

I've seen this happen time and again: when Eric speaks to someone who isn't a fan, he almost instantly wins them over. Not because of charisma, but because of his wisdom, authenticity, and the depth of his experience. The man knows what he's doing. He's more than a politician; he's a visionary. He's as real as it gets, and I say that having seen him in both his highest moments and his most vulnerable ones.

Eric's journey reflects resilience and unshakable will: from a dyslexic child to a college graduate, from being abused by a member of the force to serving twenty-two years in the NYPD, rising through the ranks until he retired as a captain. Along the way, he co-founded 100 Blacks in Law Enforcement Who Care, challenging the system from within and demanding justice for the very communities he came from. He became a New York State Senator, went on to serve as Brooklyn Borough President, and ultimately was elected Mayor of New York City. He's earned his flowers—not just for what he's accomplished, but for what he's endured.

While many politicians chase power, Eric shows up for people. He leads with conviction, not convenience. Yes, he's made mistakes, but the narrative surrounding him has been skewed, and his public image unfairly distorted. I've witnessed the passion that fuels him, and I know the heart behind the headlines.

Seeing Through the Smoke

In *Trials*, I reflect on the CBS reporter whose humanity ultimately overpowered his desire to tear me down. After I broke down during our conversation, I was able to reach him. And to my surprise, he wrote an article that wasn't harmful. It showed me that not all media is inherently evil; some still believe in the integrity of their work and aim to shed light on the truth.

But the reality is, negative press tends to overpower the good. The nature of hype-driven media: fear-mongering and fabricated controversy, has a much louder voice.

People like Katy, who bend the truth, manipulate facts, and create conflict where none exists, have contributed to the decline of legacy media. More and more, people are tuning out. They're tired of recycled narratives, tired of being bombarded with outrage, and tired of watching the truth get twisted for clicks.

We live in an age where audiences are starting to see through the noise—to recognize how easily outrage is manufactured, and how close it sits to real harm. Eventually, this cycle of sensationalism will lose its grip because people are becoming numb to it. They're beginning to crave substance over spectacle.

The public respects journalists who report with integrity and honesty, not those who are more interested in stirring the pot than telling the real story. And while the shift may take time, I believe humanity will ultimately prevail. People will see through the smoke and mirrors. And when it all plays out, those who built their careers on deception will be the ones left behind.

If this were a stage, the reporter would be the magician—controlling the spotlight, choosing the angle, and guiding the audience's gaze. Because deception doesn't just mislead; it entertains, distracts, and performs. And no one understands the art of illusion better than a magician.

Magicians thrive on distraction. To make the trick believable, they call on someone from the audience—not to expose the illusion, but to sell it. That participant, caught somewhere between nerves and awe, follows the magician's lead without question. The crowd watches, the trick lands, and the applause rolls in, all without anyone realizing how the deception was done.

This is how the media works. The trick isn't pulled off on a stage. It plays out in headlines, soundbites, and scandals. And the audience? That's you.

The press may hold the microphone, and they may have succeeded in shaping how you view Eric. But the illusion only lasts as long as you believe it.

You've seen the trick. Now, be the judge.

CHAPTER 9: LOVE AND ACCOUNTABILITY

*W*hen he called, I picked up.

It was Summer 2021, just after Eric had won the Democratic primary for New York City mayor.

Out of nowhere, my phone rang. His voice on the other end was direct. "Where are you?" he asked.

"In Pennsylvania," I told him.

"I'm in the Bronx. I just won. I need to see you."

There was urgency in his tone—a pull I couldn't ignore. Without overthinking it, I packed up, got the baby ready, and drove down to Staten Island. At this point, I hadn't spoken to Eric in years. I'd ignored him on many occasions, choosing distance when he reached out. But with this call, I found myself slipping back into the girl who never told him no.

Driving from Pennsylvania to New York, my mind was racing with thoughts about what was waiting for me. For one, aesthetically, I wasn't in the best place. I was the heaviest I had ever been—185 pounds—a stark difference from the 140-pound girl Eric had known five years earlier. Embarrassment over my appearance crept in as I gripped the wheel.

I wore a mustard-colored sweatsuit, glasses, and my hair cut short—a look that felt foreign to me since I had always worn it long. I didn't feel attractive, and the thought of seeing him again under those conditions unsettled me. Still, I kept driving, unaware that this trip would mark the beginning of an entirely new lane in my life.

I arrived at my Mom's house and found her, her husband Raul, and my grandmother sitting together in the living room. Coincidentally, they were raving about Eric and the results of the election. I joined the conversation but didn't tell them the real reason I was there. Shortly after my arrival, like clockwork, there was a knock at the door.

When he knocked, I pretended I didn't know who it was. Raul opened the door and was shocked. "Wait, oh my goodness, we were just watching you on TV!" he said. My grandmother exclaimed, "Oh my God, you're about to be mayor." Everyone was stunned to see him standing there. She even joked that I should go back upstairs and change my clothes. It's a Puerto Rican non-negotiable to always show up and look your absolute best for a man. Eric just laughed. He warmly said, "Jas doesn't need to change for anyone. She's beautiful the way she is."

That moment touched me, because it was the first time since having my daughter that anyone had made me feel beautiful. For so long, I had been uncomfortable in my own body, carrying weight I wasn't used to. But Eric's words felt different. He didn't say them out of politeness. There was truth in his voice, and I believed him.

He came inside and sat on the couch as if he belonged there, greeting everyone like family. I couldn't help but notice how good he looked. Eric was always known for his crisp shirts, and that day was no exception—he wore a clean white button-down, blue slacks, and white sneakers. He looked slimmer than I had ever seen him. In a way, it felt like we had switched places: he had lost weight, and I had gained it.

After a while, I slipped him out before my family could flood him with more questions. We laughed softly as we said our goodbyes, like two people in on a secret. Outside, I offered to drive separately, but instead, he climbed into my truck, settling in as if it were the most natural thing in the world. You know a genuine connection when a long amount of time passes, and you reunite, and it still feels like you never missed a beat. That's how you know it's timeless, and that's exactly what crossed my mind as I watched him buckle his seatbelt.

We headed to Midland Beach, parking near the pier. And then we did the thing we had always cherished most—the thing that carried us into our deepest conversations and our warmest moments. We walked.

For two hours, we talked and caught up. It felt like time had folded back on itself, leaving us suspended between the man who had just become the Democratic nominee for mayor and the man I had once loved.

We parked near the long pier that stretches for miles along Staten Island's shoreline. For me, there was something quietly remarkable about the fact that, of all the places he could have gone, Eric's first stop after winning the primary was Staten Island—the so-called "forgotten borough." It felt like a small validation, as if the borough's overlooked edges still mattered in his story, and in mine.

It was late, close to 11 p.m., when we arrived. We walked past midnight, letting the night carry us. There were no awkward silences, no hesitation. Years had passed since we'd last seen each other, but it was as though time had collapsed, and the words poured out as if no distance had ever existed. We spoke over each other, both racing to release a million thoughts in too little time, the conversation flowing as naturally as the tide brushing against the pier.

I poured ideas into him: things I thought he could do, ways to lead, ways to make the city better. He laughed, almost overwhelmed, and said, "Jas, you know so much about this city."

Some compliments hit harder than others. We live so deeply inside ourselves that when someone on the outside notices what we carry, it feels like a mirror being held up—forcing us to truly take a look. His words lit something in me. Very few people, and very few experiences, make me feel wholly myself, but walking with Eric always did. Beside him, I was in my element—fully in my skin.

We walked arm in arm along the boardwalk, the night air soft around us. Every so often, a passerby would recognize him, someone calling out, "Oh my God, Eric Adams, you just won! You're about to be mayor." There weren't many people out, maybe a dozen at most, but each voice that rang across the quiet pier was a reminder of what he had just accomplished.

He spoke about former Mayor Bloomberg—how he was mentoring him, putting him through what he called "mayor school." His gratitude in that moment was undeniable; you could hear the respect in his voice and see it in the way he recounted their conversations. But even admiration has its shadows. In June 2025, four years after that walk, Bloomberg endorsed Cuomo, Eric's opponent, and poured millions into his campaign. Eric brushed it off publicly, but privately, I could hear the crack in his voice. He admitted that people he admired had broken his heart. Bloomberg was one of them.

But that night wasn't about politics. It was about reconnection. We laughed and talked like best friends who had been apart too long. We said our goodbyes, and I drove him back to his car, unaware that those hours on the boardwalk were opening a door that had been closed for years. What felt like reconnection was, in truth, the beginning of something larger.

***

There are these "and suddenly" moments in life—moments that arrive after years of striving, reaching, and pressing against ceilings until they finally give way. Life proves it time and again: if you stay the course, breakthroughs come. Or, as Auntie Oprah likes to say, luck is preparation meeting opportunity.

Watching Eric shift from Borough President to Mayor of New York City was one of those "and suddenly" moments. One day, he was Eric, the man I knew privately. And suddenly, he was the mayor of the largest city in America. Suddenly, a motorcade waited outside. Suddenly, security flanked him wherever he went. Suddenly, his schedule was no longer his own, and every move became public.

I was deeply happy for him and proud to see the culmination of his journey. But beneath that pride lingered a quiet ache I couldn't ignore. While the world celebrated the mayor, I just wanted Eric. Not the title. Not the entourage. Not the motorcade. Just him.

After that night on the boardwalk, Eric and I began meeting for Sunday dinners. These weren't like the dates we once shared. The balance was gone. He would sit across from me and empty the weight of his week—sharing updates, frustrations, and the endless press of demands. I listened, I absorbed, and I offered what I could.

But behind that, my own reality was unraveling. I was postpartum, my emotions swinging wildly, and more often than not, my face was streaked with tears during those dinners. I was an emotional wreck, and yet I kept showing up. I couldn't understand why he had called me back into his life if he wasn't ready to pick up where we left off. I wanted clarity about my place with him, but instead, I felt like he was fitting me into his life like a missing puzzle piece—something useful, but not necessarily cherished.

And in the quiet of my heart, I knew that wasn't fair.

***

Eric won the general election in November 2021 and was sworn in as Mayor of New York City on January 1, 2022. The ink on the oath was barely dry before crisis came knocking. His first month in office was nothing short of chaos.

On January 9, just days into his tenure, a massive fire tore through the Twin Parks North West building in the Bronx. Seventeen people lost their lives, including eight children. The tragedy was one of the deadliest residential fires New York had seen in decades. Families were trapped in the smoke, huddled in stairwells and apartments that became their final resting places. The city mourned together, and in that moment, Eric was thrust into a test of leadership far sooner than anyone could have anticipated.

Less than a week later, on January 15, a woman named Michelle Go was shoved in front of an oncoming subway train in Times Square. Her death shook New Yorkers to their core and ignited a citywide conversation about mental illness and public safety.

By January 21, tragedy struck again. Just three weeks into his term, two young NYPD officers, Jason Rivera and Wilbert Mora, were shot in Harlem while responding to a domestic call. Rivera died that night, while Mora's fight ended days later. The city carried its loss like a wound, grieving them as if they were its own sons.

Eric had barely been mayor for five minutes, and already he was called to lead a grieving city through unthinkable tragedy after unthinkable tragedy. In public, he showed a brave face, commanding presence, and steady tone. But behind the podium, the man was unraveling. He was carrying a city on his back while quietly falling apart.

He was brave in responding to all of it, but there was something about Michelle Go's death that broke him. During this period, we weren't speaking. We'd had an argument, and I'd cursed him out over where we stood. But when he called in tears, before I could even unleash the anger on my tongue, he said, "No heavy stuff today, ok?"

I breathed deep, said okay, and allowed him to just break down.

There was such purity in his voice—pain and compassion, hurt and humanity, all tangled together. It was one of the rare times I saw him lay the armor down, and it reminded me that beneath the title, beneath the public image, he was still just a man carrying more than anyone should.

But even with a heart so big, navigating that responsibility is complicated. Leadership asks you to be both human and unshakable, vulnerable and unbreakable, all at once.

That contradiction doesn't diminish a person; it defines the impossible balance of public service.

***

In *The Call*, I shared the story of my work in early childhood education under Mayor Bill de Blasio—and how Universal Pre-K transformed not just my life, but the lives of thousands of families across New York City. I described the moments of hope, the power of political will, and the rare sense that policy was reaching directly into people's homes and lifting a weight off their shoulders. That experience showed me how transformative this work can be when leaders listen and act decisively.

I carried the same urgency I had felt working in education into my conversations with Eric. I warned him often that the system was slipping. Daycare centers were closing. Providers were struggling to keep their doors open. Families were losing options by the dozen. I told him repeatedly that if he didn't intervene, this would sink.

But the conversations never gained traction. My words, rooted in both data and lived experience, seemed to dissolve into the air. And in time, the city watched as dozens upon dozens of daycare centers shuttered. While Eric's administration claimed to have invested millions, the reality was that the investment wasn't timely or targeted enough to stop the bleeding. This isn't about pointing fingers; it's about understanding that leadership requires the humility to listen before a crisis erodes the progress made for those who need it most.

That's what wisdom in public service requires: valuing the insight of those closest to the work before the consequences unfold. The truth is, when you're close to someone, your perspective isn't always held in the highest regard. Eric always kept me within his circle, but not always in the way I hoped. He kept me at a respectful distance, which I could understand, because when you're a person of influence, there are countless voices in your ear. Still, it is difficult to watch someone dig a hole you know they could avoid. And that is where accountability must step in: in owning the moments when you did not listen soon enough.

Though much of the groundwork laid by the de Blasio administration eroded under Eric's leadership, I felt a spark of hope and even relief—when, in August 2025, he announced a pivotal $80 million investment in early childhood education across the city. The plan directed $70 million toward expanding pre-K special education services, including occupational and speech therapy, counseling, and support for students with disabilities. Another $10 million was dedicated to launching a pilot program that would provide free childcare for infants and toddlers from low-income families.

This funding is more than just numbers on a page; it has the potential to double the capacity of preschool assessment centers, shorten wait times for evaluations, and provide children with the services they need without forcing families to navigate endless red tape. The infant and toddler pilot, set to launch in early 2026, is a critical step toward the broader vision of universal childcare, starting with the youngest and often most vulnerable among us.

The beauty of accountability is that it doesn't end with an apology or a recognition of failure; it's followed by action. And in this case, the action has the power to shape the next generation. If this investment is nurtured, expanded, and protected, it can be a true turning point—not just for the administration, but for the families and children whose futures hang in the balance.

I will never forget the day I was told I didn't have to pay my son's tuition. The relief that washed over me was more than financial; it was the feeling that the city saw me—that it cared. Parents across New York deserve to know that same relief. Because at the end of the day, this is about children finally getting what they need, and families finally being able to breathe.

And if this city is to mean anything, let it mean that every parent, no matter their zip code or income, can one day say, "We didn't have to fight alone. Our city fought for us."

***

I wanted to write this book for a few reasons—first, to speak a truth I've been carrying for over a decade, and also to share my experiences with a world that, right now, feels incredibly turbulent. When I think about the entirety of who I am: my attitude toward life, the way I carry myself both personally and professionally, I can't help but reflect on the fact that I was raised by two incredible people.

If I stood in front of a mirror and could see beyond the reflection, I know exactly who would be staring back at me: my mother.

Growing up, my mother was militant and disciplined—the pure embodiment of tough love. Her parenting style was more rigid than nurturing, and at times, it felt like it cut deeper than it comforted. In our small apartment at 539 46th Street in Sunset Park, Brooklyn, my mom had an entire wall lined with encyclopedias. Each book was massive—some five hundred pages, others stretching into the thousands—and she had the full set, A through Z. Whenever my brother Jason and I got into trouble, she had a unique way of disciplining us.

"Alright," she'd say, her voice calm but firm, "go pick a letter and write me a five-page book report."

Yeah, you heard that right. At ten years old, we were cranking out college-length essays on whatever topic fate or the alphabet handed us. I didn't realize it at the time, but she was shaping the way my mind worked—teaching me discipline and sparking my curiosity of the world, all at once.

She reminded us recently, almost laughing at the irony, that my first report was on China, and Jason's was on computers. Looking back, it feels less like a coincidence and more like foreshadowing. My fascination with Chinese culture has only deepened over the years, influencing my worldview and even parts of my career. Jay, on the other hand, went on to land a job at the United Nations when he was just nineteen—a rare achievement—and he worked there well into his late thirties.

Not long after, I found myself walking the halls of City Hall, drawn toward public service and policy work, not fully realizing how much those encyclopedia assignments had planted the seeds for everything that would come next. In that cramped little apartment, surrounded by heavy books and heavier expectations, my mom wasn't just disciplining us; she was preparing us. Those early "punishments" became quiet investments in our futures, shaping the people we would eventually become.

I remember one of the toughest moments of my life. It was the summer of 2010. I was six months pregnant with my son, Jayden, working at the Sunset Park Redevelopment Committee (SPRC). My job as an outreach worker was to certify low-income tenants for "weatherization" improvements—things like energy-efficient appliances, new windows, and upgrades that made homes safer and more livable.

But the reality behind the work was brutal. The summer heat was relentless, and none of the residential buildings had elevators. Day after day, I climbed flight after flight of stairs, carrying 175 pounds on my frame, talking to tenants for hours in sweltering hallways where the air felt too heavy to breathe.

And beneath all of that—the heat, the stairs, the endless conversations—I was still carrying the fresh grief of my brother's accident, which had happened less than a year earlier. My body was exhausted, but so was my heart. I tried to push through, but each day became harder than the last.

Eventually, I started slipping—falling behind on my certifications, struggling to keep up with the pace. And then, finally, they let me go.

I'll never forget standing there, holding my termination letter with shaking hands, knowing I was about to bring a child into the world while navigating welfare, grief, and uncertainty all at once. It was one of the lowest points of my life—a moment where everything felt like it was collapsing around me.

I had to move back in with my mom and rebuild from the ground up. For three years straight, I put my head down and worked. I'd wake up at 3 a.m., brush my teeth, make a fresh cup of matcha, and jump straight onto my laptop at the kitchen table downstairs. At the time, my mother worked the early morning shift at Newark Airport for Continental Airlines. Her shift started at 4 a.m. sharp.

Five days a week, she'd leave the house at 3:15 a.m. on the dot—uniform pressed, bag in hand—before the sun had even risen.

I wanted her to see me at the kitchen table, grinding. I wanted her to walk through that door and know I wasn't giving up—that I was putting in the work to pull myself out of the hole I was in. It wasn't only about proving it to her. It was about proving it to myself.

In my family, welfare was taboo. It wasn't talked about, and it definitely wasn't something to be proud of. Even though I only relied on it for five months, the burden of that shame felt heavier than the bills piling up on the counter.

Still, living through it changed me. No offense is meant to anyone on assistance. I understand now, firsthand, the relief it can bring when life caves in on you. But I also saw how dangerous it can be if you stay there too long. The system, designed for temporary relief, can quietly become a trap—one that fosters dependence and rewards complacency instead of resilience.

So I sat at that table, day after day, bleary-eyed but determined, forcing myself to believe there was a way forward. Because for me, there had to be.

My mother's seriousness about life, her refusal to accept mediocrity, and her unwavering belief in discipline burned itself into me.

Her tough love turned me into someone relentless.

***

All of who we are begins in childhood. The repeated acts, the things we see, the lessons we absorb—they shape the core of who we become. Our behaviors, our attitudes, even our philosophies are modeled for us in those earliest years. That's why parents must be mindful of the seeds they plant, even in the smallest moments.

One thing I've always carried with me is my deep respect for the Black man. If you've read this book from the first page to this very moment, you know that truth by now. You've seen that I love the Black man for who he is and for what he has endured. That love was shaped early, and it became one of the deepest truths I carried into womanhood.

I give credit to my mother for that. She shielded my eyes and ears from any storms she weathered in adulthood, whether in marriage or otherwise. I grew up in a truly peaceful home. There was never any visible drama between my parents, but even if there was, my mother made sure my brother and I were unaware of it.

She respected my father enough to protect his dignity in front of his children, and in that, she taught me one of the most enduring lessons of my life: to respect a man. And when my father left, my mother never handed us her heartbreak. She reserved those feelings for her confidantes, not her children. She never gave up, never turned to a bottle or a substance, and most importantly, never lost hope. As a grown woman and a mother, I now understand what a gift that was.

Because of her example, I do my best to uplift my children's fathers in front of them, even when it's hard. She broke a cycle and, in doing so, gave me the blueprint for a different kind of strength—a quiet, steady strength. The kind that doesn't need to destroy someone to survive them.

That lesson didn't stay confined to my household. It became a compass for how I move through the world, personally and professionally. Respect does not mean blind loyalty, and love does not mean silence. The two can and must exist together.

In my personal life, it means I can stand beside a man, believe in him, and still hold him accountable when his actions fall short. In my professional life, especially in politics, it means I can admire a leader's vision and still demand they face the hard truths—not because I wish them harm, but because I want to see them victorious in ways that matter.

This is the heart of love and accountability. Just as my mother modeled respect without undermining her own boundaries, I've learned to challenge the men I respect most—not to diminish them, but to protect the people and promises they stand for. In politics, as in family, the strongest relationships aren't built on flattery or avoidance, but on truth told with care.

***

Of all Eric's sayings, none has stayed with me more than this: "Manage expectations."

At first, I thought it was his way of preparing me for inevitable disappointment—a warning that he wouldn't meet my expectations. But over time, I realized it was deeper than that.

It wasn't about failure. It was about perspective. About recognizing that everyone lives in their own reality, and those realities don't always align with yours.

It's about taking a step back, pausing before reacting, and asking yourself:

Are you mad because they fell short, or are you mad because you had unrealistic expectations?

And if it's the latter, the only person to reckon with is yourself.

Imagine your heartstrings tied to someone else's. In love, it feels effortless—like a private symphony only the two of you can hear, or a secret constellation only the two of you can see. Every glance, every touch, every word hums in perfect pitch, as if life itself has been tuned to your frequency.

But after a breakup, those same strings don't make music anymore. They buzz, they rattle, they distort. It's like a song that was once flawless, now painfully out of tune. And no matter how advanced the technology—no amount of auto-tune or digital correction can fake true harmony. What's broken in the connection can't be engineered back into alignment.

That's the hardest part to accept: the melody doesn't come back just because you want it to. You're left standing there, heart still wired to someone who's no longer plugged into you, and every movement sends static through the line. Eventually, you realize the only way to find music again is to retune yourself alone.

After my breakup with Eric, my heart closed. I've unintentionally kept myself from truly loving again since 2015. Because the strings never snapped, love never had space to return. Ten years have passed with my heart locked away, and every time an opportunity appeared, my mind refused to let it in. It's not that I haven't dated. I've had wonderful relationships over the last ten years that I cherish, and a few in particular that I was convinced would last. But falling deeply in love has remained off limits.

Was it because I once tasted a love so deep, so beautiful, so fairytale that nothing else could compare? Or is it because my heart kept holding onto expectation—the hope that one day he would finally be ready, that we could pick up where we left off so many years ago?

Whatever the reason, I couldn't allow anyone to get close enough. And yet, beneath that truth lies something even harder to admit: for over a decade, I gave everything of myself. Every "not now, Jas" was met with patience. Every request completed without hesitation. I understood the life that came with loving an influential figure. I knew it would never be traditional. But I also know I deserve more. I deserve a love that chooses me back.

Part of the reason I'm telling this story is because it's my way of letting him go. I don't want to carry this weight anymore. I've held onto it long enough—the questions, the memories, the unfinished sentences between us. I am ready to feel free.

This might seem ridiculous, but earlier this year I asked Eric to release me. He didn't even flinch before responding "no." I wasn't asked to elaborate. I wasn't even asked why. We both knew what I meant. But here, in these words, in this very moment, and for my own sanity and survival, I am releasing myself.

This isn't about holding onto hope for him. This is about choosing the love I know I deserve. I'm no longer tethered to what was or what could have been.

My heart has been tested, stretched, and broken open, but it has also healed in ways I never imagined. I've learned that repressed emotions don't vanish; they turn into stress, into weight you silently carry, into invisible chains. And I am done carrying them.

***

There is something unshakable about the connection between great loss and rain. It feels almost inevitable: when someone passes, the skies open. Over time, I found myself wondering if it's a coincidence or something greater. Since we are said to be made in His likeness, could it be that rain is God's tears, falling with ours? Whatever the case may be, rain and death seem bound together, as if the heavens insist on sharing in our grief.

It was a Saturday night—October 24, 2009. New York City was drenched in rain, and the sky was pitch black. At 7:15 p.m., I was on Zerega Ave. in the Bronx playing handball when it started, so I ran to my car to escape it. I had left my phone inside, and when I picked it up, the screen was filled with missed calls and messages. The hairs on my arms stood up. As I scanned the calls, another one came in. "Titi" flashed across the screen, and I didn't know what to expect as I picked up. It was my aunt, Pilly. Her voice was broken.

"Jas... he's dead. Jonathan died."

The words froze me. My body went stiff.

"What do you mean?" I kept asking, clinging to anything that might undo what I had just heard. But she repeated it, sobbing, her voice drowning in despair: "He died. He's gone."

I demanded to know where they were. She told me they were at Staten Island University Hospital. My mind went blank except for one thought: Get there. I flew through the rain—ninety miles an hour from the Bronx toward Staten Island. My cousin Melissa called as I went through the toll booth on the Verrazzano Bridge.

"Is it true?" she asked.

Though I was still uncertain, I told her yes.

She let out a blood-curdling scream—the kind only loss can summon. It pierced straight through me, shaking my car and searing my soul.

Of all the voices that reached for me that night, Melissa's was the one I needed to hear. Her spirit is so beautiful—steady in its goodness, carrying a calm that can ground you even in the middle of chaos. In her, there is light you can lean on, even when the world feels like it's collapsing. A call from someone like her isn't just answered; it's cherished.

When I arrived at the ER, my mother's knees gave out, and family members had to hold her up as grief overtook her body. Raul, a sergeant with the Port Authority, had been identified through the car's plate number, so when the police received notice of the accident, they called in his entire command. Officers filled the space, holding it with a reverence I can still feel.

The scene was too much for me. I wasn't crying yet; I just kept repeating, "Where is he? I need to see him." But my baby brother Jonathan was already gone. He had been declared dead on arrival and was being transferred to the morgue.

At the morgue, the ambulance was still waiting outside with my brother inside. He hadn't yet been brought in. The officers who met us spoke gently, promising, "We'll give you time before we bring him inside." But the truth was, we didn't have much time. His body had already begun to release fluids, and they needed to move him soon.

They opened the ambulance doors, and there he was: inside a black body bag, the zipper drawn up to his nose, only his closed eyes visible. My mother, Raul, and my brother Jason sat on the bench beside his body, their faces stunned, their bodies heavy with shock. I lowered myself to the floor beside his head. His stillness inside that bag was unbearable. The reality that my little brother was zipped inside it, lifeless, felt like a cruelty too sharp to name.

I leaned down and hugged his head, clinging to what little closeness I could steal back. The officer stopped me, keeping his hand on the zipper, reminding me that I wasn't allowed to pull it down to see his face. His reasoning troubled me deeply, but I listened. He was still himself to me. The warmth that lingered through the bag told me life hadn't fully left. His scent was still there, familiar and unmistakable, and what little of his face I could see looked less like death and more like sleep. It was as if he were only resting, caught somewhere between this world and the next, and I wanted to believe he might wake at any moment.

I whispered to him, "I am so proud of you. I'm so proud of you, man." I said it over and over, as if my voice could somehow carry my love into him one last time. Because it was true: I was proud of his life beyond words.

My brother lived every single day as if it were his own to conquer—full and unreserved. He was a star in every sense of the word. When the article about his death called him not only a star athlete but also a tremendous kid, they were right. Jonathan's talent knew no limits. He was exceptional at both baseball and football, already on the radar of Division I schools that saw what we had always known: he was destined for greatness.

But it wasn't just the sports. It was the way the room came alive when he walked in. His presence lit up every space he entered. Anyone would tell you he was the heartbeat of his school. They called him Johnny Ray with affection—the one who could play any game, make the teachers laugh, and still be the brightest light in every crowd.

As word of the crash spread, people began gathering outside my mother's house. They didn't yet know that Jonathan hadn't made it. When they were told, the ground seemed to break open. His teammates sobbed so hard they collapsed onto the pavement. Some hurled. Some screamed. The night filled with cries that seemed to echo up to the sky.

I stood a little apart, watching it all as if I were float-ing outside my own body. And then, as if grief needed a sharper blade, I saw it: the pickup truck towing the car Jonathan had crashed in. It rolled slowly past the house, rain dripping off its mangled frame. That sight ripped something open in me. I screamed and fell apart, my uncle Melo wrapping his arms around me, whispering, "Don't look, Jas. Don't look."

But I had already seen it. That broken car told the story my heart was refusing to accept.

From the night of the accident until the day of the funeral, grief hollowed me out. I refused to shower because I had his blood under my fingernails. Eventually, my friends forced me into a warm bathtub, rubbing my back as I sobbed, watching the blood wash away. The anxiety attacks returned with vengeance. I couldn't drive, couldn't focus, couldn't eat. I lost twenty pounds in a matter of days, my body shrinking until I looked like a shadow of myself. I was so small that on the day of the service, none of my clothes fit, so I wore one of Jonathan's hoodies cinched with a belt, along with a pair of pants that barely clung to me.

Jonathan's services were held at International Christian Center— ICC, as we called it—on Richmond Ave., and more than 4,000 people came to pay their respects. The turnout was so overwhelming that officials had to close a portion of the avenue. Cars poured into the streets, people lined the sidewalks, and the entire community seemed to stretch itself open in mourning. It felt like the city itself had stopped to acknowledge that Jonathan Ray was gone.

Amid all the crowds, the flowers, and the prayers, none of it softened the one moment I feared most.

When the time came to close the casket, I wasn't ready. I couldn't accept it. I kept talking to him, clinging as if my words could call him back. They told me it was time, but I begged them to wait. The finality was too much. Eventually, they had to pull me away as the casket was taken outside.

My grief cracked me open. I screamed, sobbing uncontrollably. Shawn Stratford, the funeral director who had cared for Jonathan, wrapped his arms around me, whispering for me to calm down. But I couldn't. My body convulsed in a sorrow too big to contain.

When the casket finally closed, something shifted inside me. I felt the energy of earth and all of creation surge through me like electricity, until it seemed as though the church itself was shaking.

That moment changed my life. It was my introduction to the search for answers: the eternal "why."

Why am I here? What is life even about? What is my purpose? Why did this happen?

One day, two weeks before his death, my brother stood in our mother's kitchen, locked in a debate about scripture. He and my mother went back and forth over the words of John 16:5-7, each determined to get it right. This was 2009, before we could just pull a phone from our pocket and search for the answer in seconds. Their voices rose and fell with passion while I was distracted, only half-listening.

After his passing, we returned to that very scripture he had been so intent on recalling. When we read the words, it sent chills through us:

"Now I am going to Him who sent me, yet none of you asks me, 'Where are you going?' But because I have said these things, you are filled with grief. Nevertheless, I tell you the truth: it is for your good that I am going away. Unless I go away, the Counselor will not come to you; but if I go, I will send him to you."

We placed those words on his funeral card—a scripture that became both a reminder and a comfort. It felt, in some spiritual way, as though Jonathan had been preparing us, even if unknowingly. His relentless search to quote that verse became a message left behind—one that I will carry with me for the rest of my life.

When I think about the hardest moments of my life, nothing compares to losing my brother at just sixteen years old. Sixteen is supposed to be the beginning, not the end. Sixteen is for first loves, Friday night lights, and dreams that still stretch as wide as the sky. And yet, in an instant, his life was gone.

That loss has been the driving force behind my persistence, my discipline, and my refusal to quit. His life reminded me that the only way to honor him is to live unafraid.

To a certain extent, I enjoyed the freedom I had in the bliss of young ignorance. But Jonathan's death broke me and lifted the veil. It anchored me in both reality and resilience, forcing me to face life stripped of illusions. Through every storm, every heartbreak, every test, I've carried that strength forward.

And in his honor, I will endure.

***

To be from New York is to know the world's chaos and still find your voice in it. To be American is to believe that the promise—no matter how battered—is still worth holding onto. As former presidential candidate Vivek Ramaswamy once said, "America is founded on our humanity... that we can believe and aspire to something we will inevitably fall short of." That, to me, is the essence of **political humanity**: holding space for imperfection while still daring to believe.

I love my city. I love my country. And I believe our flaws don't erase our promise. But make no mistake about it: we are in a fight for the soul of America.

In the fall of 2022, I found myself facing a moment that would redefine how I understood strength and humanity. In a Kohl's parking lot in Mariner's Harbor, Staten Island, a dispute over a parking space escalated until a woman—my age, my hue, my sis in every visible way—punched me in the face.

As I mentioned earlier, I am a fourth-degree black belt. Fighting, to me, is not only a sport; it is a welcome exchange. A natural response in the heat of that moment. But immediately after the first drop of blood fell from my nose, her male companion shouted:

"What are you doing? You're pregnant!"

She wasn't visibly pregnant, so I imagine she was still in her first term. With my 12-year-old son watching his mother being assaulted, I realized I had a choice: I could retaliate—to show my son how tough I was, to prove the stories of my martial arts days weren't just legend—and I could perpetuate the cycle of violence. Or I could be the one to stop it.

In that split second, I thought about the unborn child, the innocent life involved, and my own child standing beside me. I realized the true act of courage wasn't in fighting back; it was in walking away. And so, blood still dripping from my nose, I chose to leave the conflict behind.

That moment taught me something profound. First, I wasn't angry anymore. I'd done my fair share of responding with aggression, but this time, I wanted a different outcome. It showed me that in a world where we're fighting for the soul of our city and our country, someone has to be the one to break the chain of retaliation.

If there's one lesson from this book, it's that we need to see each other as human—to love our enemies, as Luke 6 suggests—and to be the ones who choose peace over vengeance. Our humanity and our survival depend on it.

When this is all over, people will say what they want about me. Excerpts will be pulled, headlines will be written, and narratives about me and Eric will be shaped. Opinions will fly. Fiction will land. But this book isn't about control; it's about truth. The messy, complicated, inconvenient kind.

I've often thought about the old saying: "First they love you, then they hate you, then they love you again." I've watched Eric live it. And maybe that's the point: life in the public eye rises and falls with perception, but perception is never the whole story. Somewhere beneath the noise, there's the humanity we all share.

I wrote this book because I believe we need a new way forward—beyond cancel culture—toward something closer to **accountability with compassion**. Call it grace culture, if you want: the belief that people are more than their worst mistakes. That only death should be final, and even that is debatable.

Jonathan's death taught me that pain can undo you, but it can also rebuild you if you let it. Eric taught me that intimacy exists in gray spaces, in contradictions, in truths we can't always defend. And yes, I loved him with a fullness I may never feel again. That love, flawed and complicated as it was, was worth living for.

And yet, here I stand—willing to lay my heart bare and my reputation on the line to test the strength of my voice. Because that's who I've always been: a risk taker, a dreamer, a doer. You don't escape trauma by ignoring it. You face it. You name it. And you reclaim it.

At first glance, the cover of this book may look like a tell-all, something meant to stir scandal. But take a closer look, and you'll see it's a symbol of protection. In our closest moments, I would rub the back of Eric's head, where his old surgery scar left him vulnerable. He could sit still for hours if I kept my hand there, as if my touch eased something no one else could reach. Old scars don't always cause deep pain, but they remain sensitive. And when touched, they can bring comfort and relief.

In a time when masculinity is under fire and accountability so easily slips into humiliation, I've searched for balance—for that sacred space where truth and dignity can coexist. Sometimes, the most radical act is to shield that vulnerability and protect each other's humanity, even when disappointment cuts deep.

I can't control how this story is received. What matters is what you carry from these pages—the courage to believe again, the grace to forgive, and the resilience to show up and keep hope alive.

Political Humanity isn't about power or perception. It's about choosing to see the person beneath the title, the headline, the mistake. It's about remembering that we all have the choice to let our pain break us—or define us. Everyone is given a choice in how they want to reemerge.

What comes next—for me, for our city, and for our country—remains unwritten.

We'll have to unpack that in the next book.